THE

MOUSE

THAT

ROARED

Culture and Education Series

Series Editors: Henry A. Giroux, Pennsylvania State University
Joe L. Kincheloe, Pennsylvania State University

THE
MOUSE
THAT
ROARED

Disney and the End of Innocence

Henry A. Giroux

ROWMAN & LITTLEFIELD PUBLISHERS, INC.
Lanham • Boulder • New York • Oxford

ROWMAN & LITTLEFIELD PUBLISHERS, INC.

Published in the United States of America
by Rowman & Littlefield Publishers, Inc.
4720 Boston Way, Lanham, Maryland 20706

12 Hid's Copse Road
Cumnor Hill, Oxford OX2 9JJ, England

British Library Cataloguing in Publication Information Available

The hardback edition of this book was catalogued by the Library of
Congress as follows:

Giroux, Henry A.
    The mouse that roared : Disney and the end of innocence / Henry A.
Giroux.
        p.   cm.
    Includes bibliographical references and index.
    1. Walt Disney Company—History.   2. Popular culture—United
States.   I. Title.
PN1999.W27G57   1999
384'.8'06579494—dc21   99-11241
                                                                  CIP

ISBN 0-8476-9109-8 (cloth : alk. paper)
ISBN 0-8476-9110-1 (paper : alk. paper)

Printed in the United States of America

∞ ™ The paper used in this publication meets the minimum
requirements of American National Standard for Information
Sciences—Permanence of Paper for Printed Library Materials, ANSI
Z39.48–1992.

For Susan, who is always in my heart.

For Jonathan Kozol, who is a national resource and the public conscience for the plight of children.

For Leo DiMeo, who took me under his wing when I was a kid and "saved" my life along with countless others who came from families and neighborhoods that few people believed in or cared about.

CONTENTS

ACKNOWLEDGMENTS

A number of people were crucial in reading or giving me advice about various aspects of this book. I want to thank Stanley Aronowitz, Roger Simon, Carol Becker, Andrew Ross, Mike Hill, Ken Saltman, David Trend, Jeff Nealon, David Theo Goldberg, Peter McLaren, Barry Kanpol, Lawrence Grossberg, Donaldo Macedo, Pat Shannon, Heidi Hendershott, Valerie Janesick, Imre Szeman, Ron Bettig, Eric Weiner, Don Schule, Jergen Neubauer, and Michaela Amato.

I thank my wife, Susan Searls Giroux, for reading and editing every page of this book. This book is dedicated to her for her love, intelligence, and passion. My boys, Jack, Brett, and Chris, were a great resource for me in learning how young children mediate, resist, and question Disney culture. Thanks, guys. This book is also for Grizz, who is always there with such love.

I am also fortunate to have had a wonderful editor and friend, Dean Birkenkamp, who provided support and numerous insights in helping me write this book.

Earlier and much different versions of two of these chapters appeared in the *Socialist Review*.

There is nothing innocuous left. The little pleasures, expressions of life that seemed exempt from the responsibility of thought, not only have an element of deviant silliness, of callous refusal to see, but directly serve their diametrical opposite.

—Theodor Adorno, *Minima Moralia*

INTRODUCTION: DISNEY'S
TROUBLED UTOPIA

> The Disney stores promote the consumer products,
> which promote the theme parks, which promote the
> TV shows. The TV shows promote the company. Roger
> Rabbit promotes Christmas at Disneyland.
>
> —Michael D. Eisner, chairman, CEO, and
> president of the Walt Disney Company

Within two days after Mark McGwire belted his sixty-second home run, breaking Roger Maris's record, a television ad ran on all the major networks in which McGwire appeared hitting the home run, jogging around the bases, and picking up his son in celebration of his record-breaking event. A camera zoomed in on McGwire, hero to millions of kids, holding his son in his arms, and a voice asked: "What are you going to do now?" McGwire smiled, looked directly at the camera, and replied, "I am going to take my son to Disneyland."

Following the McGwire ad, the dominant media, including the three major television network news programs, announced that the groundskeeper who had picked up McGwire's record-setting baseball would give it back to him and that this generous deed would be rewarded with a free round-trip ticket to Disneyworld. Once again, Disney managed to appropriate a high-profile American image and turn it into an advertisement for corporate America.

The organization and regulation of culture by large corporations such as Disney profoundly influence children's culture and their everyday lives. The concentration of control over the means of producing, circulating, and exchanging information has been matched by the emergence of new technologies that have transformed culture, especially popular culture, which is the primary way in which youth learn about themselves, their relationship to others, and the larger world. The Hollywood film industry, television, satellite broadcasting technologies, the internet, posters, magazines, billboards, newspapers, videos, and other media forms and technologies have transformed culture into a pivotal force, "shaping human meaning and behavior and regulat[ing] our social practices at every turn."[1]

Although the endlessly proliferating media sites seem to promise unlimited access to vast stores of information, such sites are increasingly controlled by a handful of multinational corporations. Consider the Disney Company's share of the communication industry. Disney's numerous holdings include a controlling interest in twenty television stations that reach 25 percent of U.S. households; ownership of over twenty-one radio stations and the largest radio network in the United States, serving 3,400 stations and covering 24 percent of all households in the country; three music studios; the ABC television network; and five motion picture studios. Other holdings include, but are not limited to, television and cable channels, book publishing, sports teams, theme parks, insurance companies, magazines, and multimedia productions.[2]

Mass-produced images fill our daily lives and condition our most intimate perceptions and desires. At issue for parents, educators, and others is how culture, especially media culture, has become a substantial, if not the primary, educational force in regulating the meanings, values, and tastes that set the norms that offer up and legitimate particular subject positions—what it means to claim an identity as a male, female, white, black, citizen, noncitizen. The media culture defines childhood, the national past, beauty, truth, and social agency.[3] The impact of new electronic technologies as teaching machines can be seen in some rather astounding statistics. It is estimated that "the average American spends more than four hours a day watching television. Four hours a day, 28 hours a week, 1456 hours a year."[4] The American Medical Association reports that the "number of hours spent in front of a television or video screen is the single biggest chunk of time in the waking life of an American child."[5]

Such statistics warrant grave concern, given that the pedagogical messages provided through such programming are shaped largely by a $130-billion-a-year advertising industry, which sells not only its products but also values, images, and identities that are largely aimed at teaching young people to be consumers. It would be reductionist not to recognize that there is also some excellent programming that is provided to audiences, but by and large much of what is produced on television and in the big Hollywood studios panders to the lowest common denominator, defines freedom as consumer choice, and debases public discourse by reducing it to spectacle.[6]

Consider the enormous control that a handful of transnational corporations have over the diverse properties that shape popular and media culture: "51 of the largest 100 economies in the world are corporations."[7] Moreover, the U.S. media is dominated by fewer than ten conglomerates, whose annual sales range from $10 billion to $27 billion. These include major corporations such as Time-Warner, General Electric, Disney, Viacom, TCI, and Westinghouse. Not only are these firms major producers of much of the entertainment and news, culture, and information that permeates our daily lives, they also produce "media software and have distribution networks like television networks, cable channels and retail stores."[8]

Although this book focuses on the role that the Disney corporation in particular plays as an educational force in shaping American popular culture, it also makes clear that the production of meaning, social practices, and desires—or what can be called public pedagogy—must be addressed as both an educational issue and a matter of politics and institutional power. Although my focus is on Disney's cultural politics and its attempt to mystify its corporate agenda with appeals to fun, innocence, and purity, the seriousness of the political and economic threat that Disney and other corporations present to a democracy because of their control over information and their monopoly over the regulation of public space cannot be underestimated.

I don't suggest that Disney is engaged in a conspiracy to undermine American youth or democracy around the world. Nor do I suggest that Disney is part of an evil empire incapable of providing joy and pleasure to the millions of kids and adults who visit its theme parks, watch its videos and movies, and buy products from its toy stores. On the contrary, the main issue here is that such entertainment now takes place under conditions "in which the media becomes a critical site for the articulation of a major intellectual shift in the ground of public discourse . . . in which pricing systems are now brought to bear on any problem, any time, anywhere."[9] In other words, media conglomerates such as Disney are not merely producing harmless entertainment, disinterested news stories, and unlimited access to the information age; nor are they removed from the realm of power, politics, and ideology. But recognition of the pleasure that Disney provides should not blind us to the realization that Disney is about more than entertainment.

I also do not suggest that the effect of Disney films, radio stations, theme parks, magazines, and other products is the same for all those who are exposed to them. Disney is not a self-contained system of unchanging formal conventions. Disney culture, like all cultural formations, is riddled with contradictions; rather than being a monolithic empire, the Disney culture offers potentially subversive moments and pleasures in a range of contradictory and complex experiences. In fact, any approach to studying Disney must address the issue of why so many kids and adults love Disney and experience its theme parks, plays, and travel opportunities as a counterlogic that allows them to venture beyond the present while laying claim to unrealized dreams and hopes.

For adults, Disney's theme parks offer an invitation to adventure, a respite from the drudgery of work, and an opportunity to escape from the alienation of daily life. As Susan Willis points out, Disney invites adults to construct a new sense of agency founded on joy and happiness and to do so by actively participating in their own pleasure, whether it be a wedding ceremony, a cruise ship adventure, or a weekend at the Disney Institute.[10] Disney's appeal to pleasure and the "child in all of us" is also rooted in a history that encompasses the lives of many baby boomers. These adults have grown up with the Disney culture and often "discover some nostalgic connection to [their] childhood" when they enter into the Disney cultural apparatus. In this sense, Disney can be thought of as an "immense nostalgia machine whose staging and specific attractions are generationally coded to strike a chord with the various age categories of its guests."[11] Disney's power lies, in part, in its ability to tap into the lost hopes, abortive dreams, and utopian potential of popular culture.

Disney's appeal to fantasy and dreams becomes more powerful when played out against a broader American landscape in which cynicism has become a permanent fixture. Disney's invitation to a world in which "the fun always shines" does more than invoke the utopian longing and promise of the sun-drenched vacation. It also offers an acute sense of the extraordinary in the ordinary, a powerful antidote to even the most radical forms of pessimism. But, at the same time, Disney's utopia points beyond the given while remaining firmly within it. As the philosopher Ernst Bloch points out, genuine wishes are felt here at the start, but these are often siphoned off within constructions of nostalgia, fun, and childhood innocence that undercut the utopian dream of "something else"—that which extends beyond what the market and a commodity-crazed society can offer.[12]

And yet, even in this "swindle of fulfillment"[13] there are contradictions in the way adults experience a Disney culture that combines pleasure and irritation, subordination and resistance, and genuine affective involvement and passive identification. For example, Disney's invitation to adult couples to experience an erotic fling—an escape into a hoped-for rekindling of sensual desire and pleasure by taking a vacation at one of Disney's theme parks—is undermined by an environment that is antiseptic, homogeneous, regulated, and controlled. And yet this exoticizing of the Disney landscape does contain a utopian element that exceeds the reality of the Disney-produced commercialized spaces in which such desires find their origins as well as their finale in the fraudulent promise of satisfaction.

For children, Disney is a wish-landscape that combines fantasy, fun, and the opportunity to enter into a more colorful and imaginary world. Its animated films usher children into terrains that are exotic and other—filled with the fantasies of escape, romantic adventures, and powerful emotional themes about survival, separation, death, and loss—and provide points of identification and the capacity to mediate and experience in fantasy form realities that children have not yet encountered. Disney's theme parks invoke the romantic fantasy of escaping the discipline and regulation of school, the fascination and magic of grotesquely shaped Disney characters, the adventure of hidden spaces, and the thrill of park rides. Disney offers children the opportunity to dream, vindicating the necessity of fantasies that contain utopian traces and that offer an antidote to the brutality and emptiness of everyday life. But like all dreams, the dreams that Disney provides for children are not innocent and must be interrogated for the futures they envision, the values they promote, and the forms of identifications they offer.

There are no passive dupes in this script, and many of Disney's texts offer opportunities for opposite readings. But at the same time, the potential for subversive readings, the recognition of the complex interplay of agency, and the mixture of alienation and pleasure that the culture industry promotes do not cancel out the power of a corporation like Disney to monopolize the media and saturate everyday life with its own ideologies. Although it is true that people mediate what they see, buy, wear, and consume and bring different meanings to the texts and products that companies like Disney produce, it is crucial that any attempt to deal with the relationship between culture and politics not stop with such a recognition but investigate both its limits and its strengths, particularly in dealing with the three- to eight-year-old crowd.[14]

Although media and popular culture are contested terrains, always subject to disruptive translations and negotiations, it would be a political and pedagogical mistake to affirm the "active and critical element in popular cultural usages, [while] overlooking the overwhelming historical realities of inequality and subordination that condition [such responses]."[15] My interpretation of Disney culture is not meant to be static or universal but a pedagogical attempt to challenge both the diverse meanings and the common-sense renderings that we bring to our encounter with Disney culture. Simultaneously, I wish to interrogate the historical, institutional, and political conditions that shape, limit, and condition such mediations.

My goal is to offer readers a set of tools that enable them to inquire into what Disney represents, in a way that they might not have thought about, and to shatter common-sense assumptions regarding Disney's claim to both promoting fun and games and protecting childhood innocence. In short, I want both to challenge and to go beyond the charge that cultural critics who take a critical stand on Disney or argue for a particular interpretation of what Disney culture represents fail to consider other possible readings of Disney texts or "simply offer self-righteous tirades against an endless litany of 'isms.' "[16]

In fact, the real issue may not be ideological rigidity on the part of progressive cultural critics or their failure to assign multiple interpretations to Disney's texts but rather the problem of how to read cultural forms as they articulate with a whole assemblage of other texts, ideologies, and practices. How audiences interpret Disney's texts may not be as significant as how some ideas, meanings, and messages under certain political conditions become more highly valued as representations of reality than others—and further, how these representations assume the force of ideology by making an appeal to common sense while at the same time shaping political policies and programs that serve very specific interests, such as the 1996 Telecommunications Act and the forging of school–business partnerships.

For some cultural theorists, the strength of Disney's texts lies in the potential they have for pleasure and in the multiple readings—outside of the realm of ideology—they provide for diverse audiences. Granted the importance of recognizing that reception is itself constitutive of how meaning is produced and that the work of conferring meaning cannot be specified in advance, it is not an insight that by default eliminates the inordinate power of megacorporations such as Disney to control the range of meanings that circulate within society. There is a difference between, on the one hand, political formations that involve a mix of institutional and ideological forces and, on the other, reading methods that remind us that the relationship between determinations and effects is problematic. Edward Said makes an important point about the relationship between method and politics when he insists that some theorists "have fallen into the trap of believing that method is sovereign and can be systematic without also acknowledging that method is always part of some larger ensemble of relationships headed and moved by authority and power."[17]

For Said, the forces of cultural production and reception are not equal, which suggests that we should deal very differently with politics, power, and pedagogy in linking these two modes of intervention. Focusing on how we interpret, mediate, or resist different messages, products, and social practices does not cancel out the concentrated power that produces them, nor does it address the broader historical, cultural, and institutional affiliations that often privilege texts with specific intentions and meanings. Nor does such a method suggest that one is actually working out of a political project that takes a stand against particular forms of domination while struggling to expand democratic relations and pluralize democratic public spheres. What is any method, including audience research (in its various manifestations), actually against? What is the political project that gives it meaning? And how does this appeal to method address the growing concentration of political and economic power and the broad spectrum of texts, institutions, and social practices that corporations such as Disney reproduce?

Yet how people mediate texts, produce different readings of cultural forms, and allow themselves to experience the pleasure of Disney culture cannot be ignored. However, the ways in which such messages, products, and conventions "work" on audiences is one that must be left open to the investigation of particular ethnographic interventions and pedagogical practices. There is no virtue, ideologically or politically, in simply pronouncing what Disney means, as if that is all there is to do. I am suggesting a very different approach to Disney, one that highlights the pedagogical and the contextual by raising questions about Disney itself, what role it plays (1) in shaping public memory, national identity, gender roles, and childhood values; (2) in suggesting who qualifies as an American; and (3) in determining the role of consumerism in American life. These questions expand the scope of inquiry, allowing us to enter into such a discussion in a way that we ordinarily might not. Disney needs to be engaged as a public discourse, and doing so means offering an analysis that forces civic discourse and popular culture to rub against each other. Such an engagement represents both a pedagogical intervention and a way of recognizing the changing contexts in which any text must be understood and engaged.

Questioning what Disney teaches is part of a much broader inquiry regarding what it is parents, children, educators, and others need to know in order to critique and challenge, when necessary, those institutional and cultural forces that have a direct impact on public life. Such inquiry is most important at a time when corporations hold such an inordinate amount of power in shaping children's culture into a largely commercial endeavor, using their various cultural technologies as teaching machines to commodify and homogenize all aspects of everyday life—and in this sense posing a potential threat to the real freedoms associated with a substantive democracy. But questioning what megacorporations such as Disney teach also means appropriating the most resistant and potentially subversive ideas, practices, and images at work in their cultural productions.

This book takes as its main tenet that what Disney teaches cannot be abstracted from a number of larger questions: What does it mean to make corporations accountable to the public? How do we link public pedagogy to a critical democratic view of citizenship? How do we develop forms of critical education that enable young people and adults to become aware of and interrogate the media as a major political, pedagogical, and social force? At the very least, such a project suggests developing educational programs, both within and outside of schools, that offer students the opportunity to learn how to use and critically read the new media technologies and their cultural productions. Organizing to democratize the media and make it accountable to a participating citizenry also demands engaging in the hard political and pedagogical task of opening up corporations such as Disney to public interrogation and critical dialogue.[18]

Disney's overwhelming presence in the United States and abroad reminds us that the battle over culture is central to the struggle over meaning and institutional power and that, for learning to become meaningful, critical, and emancipatory, it must not be surrendered to the dictates of consumer choice or to a prohibition on critical engagements with how ideologies work within cultural discourses. On the contrary, critical learning must be linked to the empowering demands of social responsibility, public accountability, and critical citizenship.

How we educate our youth is related to the collective future embodied in the stories that are told in the noncommodified spheres of our public culture. As noncommodified public culture comes under assault, we are faced with a growing commercial sphere that profoundly limits the vocabulary and imagery available for defining, defending, and reforming the state, civil society, and public culture as centers for critical learning and citizenship. None of us stands outside of the cultures of pleasure and entertainment that now hold such sway over American society. The test of such cultures may not lie in whether they are capable of producing joy and merriment but rather in their capacity to offer narratives of pleasure without undermining the basic institutions of democracy. What we don't need is a culture industry that increasingly produces stories that turn children's desires and dreams into fodder for the Disney imagineers—and into profits for the Disney Stores and power-lunch brokers.

NOTES

1. Stuart Hall, "The Centrality of Culture: Notes on the Cultural Revolutions of Our Time," in Kenneth Thompson, ed., *Media and Cultural Regulation* (Thousand Oaks, Calif.: Sage, 1997), p. 232.

2. Mark Crispin Miller and Janine Jacquet Biden, "The National Entertainment State," *Nation*, June 3, 1996, pp. 23–26.

3. The concentrated power of the media market by corporations is evident in the following figures: "In cable, Time Warner and TCI control 47.4 percent of all subscribers; in radio, Westinghouse, in addition to owning the CBS television network, now owns 82 radio stations; in books, Barnes & Noble and Borders sell 45 percent of all books in the United States. . . . three studios share 57 percent of the overall market. In newspapers, only 24 cities compared to 400 fifty years ago support two or more daily newspapers." Robert W. McChesney, "Global Media for the Global Economy," in Don Hazen and Julie Winokur, eds., *We the Media* (New York: New Press, 1997), p. 27.

4. Hazen and Winokur, *We the Media*, p. 64.

5. Ibid., p. 64.

6. Pierre Bourdieu's analysis of the systemic corruption of television in France is equally informative when applied to the United States. See Pierre Bourdieu, *On Television,* translated by Priscilla Parkhurst Ferguson (New York: New Press, 1998).

7. Joshua Karliner, "Earth Predators," *Dollars and Sense* (July/ August 1998), p. 7.

8. Robert W. McChesney, *Corporate Media and the Threat to Democracy* (New York: Seven Stories Press, 1997), p. 18. There is an enormous amount of information on the new global conglomerates and their effects on matters of democracy, censorship, free speech, social policy, national identity, and foreign policy. For example, see classics such as Herbert I. Schiller, *Culture Inc.: The Corporate Takeover of Public Expression* (New York: Oxford University Press, 1989); Noam Chomsky, *Manufacturing Consent* (New York: Pantheon, 1988); Ben H. Bagdikian, *The Media Monopoly,* 4th ed. (Boston: Beacon, 1992); George Gerbner and Herbert I. Schiller, eds., *Triumph of the Image* (Boulder, Colo.: Westview, 1992); Douglas Kellner, *Television and the Crisis of Democracy* (Boulder, Colo.: Westview, 1990); Philip Schlesinger, *Media, State and Nation* (London: Sage, 1991); John Fiske, *Media Matters* (Minneapolis: University of Minnesota Press, 1994); Jeff Cohen and Norman Solomon, *Through the Media Looking Glass* (Monroe, Me.: Common Courage Press, 1995); Erik Barnouw, *Conglomerates and the Media* (New York: New Press, 1997).

9. Toby Miller, *Technologies of Truth* (Minneapolis: University of Minnesota Press, 1998), p. 90.

10. Susan Willis, "Problem with Pleasure," in Susan Willis, Jane Kuenz, Karen Klugman, and Shelton Waldrep, eds., *Inside the Mouse: Work and Play at Disney World* (Durham: Duke University Press, 1995).

11. Ibid., p. 5.

12. Ernst Bloch, *The Utopian Function of Art and Literature*, translated by Jack Zipes and Frank Mecklenburg (Cambridge: MIT Press, 1988); Ernst Bloch, *The Principle of Hope*, vol. 1, translated by Neville Plaice, Stephen Plaice, and Paul Knight (Cambridge: MIT Press, 1986).

13. Anson Rabinach, "Unclaimed Heritage: Ernst Bloch's *Heritage of Our Times* and the Theory of Fascism," *New German Critique* (Spring 1977), p. 8.

14. I am invoking Meghan Morris's argument in which she identifies the chief error of cultural studies to be the narcissistic identity "between the knowing subject of cultural studies, and a collective subject, the 'people.' " The people in this discourse "have no necessary defining characteristics—except an indomitable capacity to 'negotiate' readings, generate new interpretations, and remake the materials of culture. . . . So against the hegemonic force of the dominant classes, 'the people' in fact represent the most creative energies and functions of critical reading. In the end they are not simply the cultural student's object of study, [but] his native informants. The people are also the textually delegated, allegorical emblem of the critic's own activity." "Banality in Cultural Studies," *Discourse* 10:2 (1988), p. 17.

15. Francis Mulhern, "The Politics of Cultural Studies," *Monthly Review* 47:3 (1995), p. 38.

16. A classic example of this type of critique is David Buckingham, "Dissin' Disney: Critical Perspectives on Children's Media Culture," *Media, Culture, and Society* 19 (1997), p. 290.

17. Edward W. Said, *The World, the Text, and the Critic* (Cambridge: Harvard University Press, 1983), p. 169.

18. On another political register, expanding democratic public

culture means working to get organized labor and progressive social movements to forge partnerships and pool their intellectual and material resources in order to create alternative public spheres in which democratic identities, relations, and values can flourish. Such partnerships would offer multiple sites of resistance to a culture industry such as Disney in which the call for innocence, happiness, and unity appears to be "transformed into a prohibition on thinking itself." Theodor W. Adorno, *Critical Models: Interventions and Catchwords,* translated by Henry W. Pickford (New York: Columbia University Press, 1998), p. 290.

I

DISNEY AND THE POLITICS OF PUBLIC CULTURE

I think of a child's mind as a blank book. During the
first years of his life, much will be written on the pages.
The quality of that writing will affect his life profoundly.

—Walt Disney

THE ECLIPSE OF CHILDHOOD INNOCENCE

In the popular mind, Walt Disney, the man and the company, has become synonymous with the notion of childhood innocence. As suburban America witnesses urban violence invading its schools, homes, and neighborhoods,
Disney becomes a symbol for the security and romance of
the small-town America of yesteryear—a pristine never-
never land in which children's fantasies come true, happiness reigns, and innocence is kept safe through the magic
of pixie dust.

Of course, Walt realized that innocence as a cultural metaphor had to be associated with a particular rendering of
childhood as well as a specific view of the American past,

present, and future. In other words, Disney's view of innocence had to be constructed within particular maps of meaning in which children and adults could define themselves through a cultural language that offers them both modest pleasure and a coherent sense of identity. This suggested that Disney define innocence as part of the logic of home entertainment and also, pedagogically, as a set of values and practices that associate the safeguarding of childhood with a strong investment in the status quo and in the market as a sphere of consumption. Refusing to separate entertainment from education, Disney challenged the assumption that entertainment has little educational value and is simply about leisure. For Walt Disney, education was not confined to schools but implicit in the broader realm of popular culture and its own mechanisms for the production of knowledge and values. He also knew that it had to be lively and enjoyable.

Walt's fusing of entertainment and education blurred the boundaries between public culture and commercial interests and found expression both in the attractions that came to characterize theme parks such as Disneyland and Disney World and in the extended range of cultural and media outlets that shape everyday life. Hollywood films, radio stations, television networks, sports franchises, book publishing, and daily newspapers provided the Disney Company with sites from which to promote its cultural pedagogy. Walt Disney's key insight was that the educational field could be reconstructed and transformed through the mastery of new spaces for leisure, new electronic technologies, and new global markets. Pedagogy, for Disney, was not restricted to schooling, and schooling did not strictly define the contexts in which children could learn, make affective investments, and reconstruct their identities.

If we imagine the Disney Company as a teaching machine whose power and influence can, in part, be measured by the number of people who come in contact with its goods, messages, values, and ideas, it becomes clear that Disney wields enormous influence on the cultural life of the nation, especially with regard to the culture of children. Consider that "more than 200 million people a year watch a Disney film or home video, 395 million watch a Disney TV show every week; 212 million listen or dance to Disney music, records, tapes or compact discs. . . . More than 50 million people a year from all lands pass through the turnstiles of Disney theme parks."[1] In the company's *1997 Annual Report,* Michael Eisner, chairman and chief executive officer of the Walt Disney Company, claimed that during the week of November 2–8, 1997, Disney culture attracted the attention of the following numbers of people, mostly children: "During these seven days, 34.2 million people watched *The Wonderful World of Disney,* 3.3 million people turned on *One Saturday Morning,* 3.8 million subscribers viewed the Disney Channel, 2.8 million listened to Radio Disney, 793,000 visited Disney theme parks, 810,000 made a purchase at a Disney store and nine million copies of *Beauty and the Beast: The Enchanted Christmas* were shipped to video stores across the country."[2]

Disney's commercial success is a testimonial to the crucial role that culture and entertainment play "in the structure and organization of late-modern society, in the processes of development of the global environment and in the disposition of its economic and material resources."[3] Disney's success represents, in part, the power of the culture industries to mediate and influence almost every aspect of our lives. But Disney's emergence as part of a new entertainment monopoly also points to the ways in which corporate culture uses its power as an educational force to redefine the relationship between childhood and innocence, citizenship and consumption, civic values and commercial values. How children learn and what they learn, in a society in which power is increasingly held by megacorporations, raises serious concerns about what noncommodified public spheres exist to safeguard children from the ravages of a market logic that provides neither a context for moral considerations nor a language for defending vital social institutions and policies as a public good.

A democratic culture fulfills one of its most important functions when it views children as a social investment, whose worth and value cannot be measured exclusively in commercial and private terms. That is, a democratic culture provides the institutional and symbolic resources necessary for young people to develop their capacities to engage in critical thought, participate in power relations and policy decisions that affect their lives, and transform those racial, social, and economic inequities that close down democratic social relations.[4]

The concept of innocence, when linked to the notion of social justice, references the obligation for a society to hold adults responsible for creating institutions in which education is viewed as a public asset and not merely a private good. In this context, the requirements of citizenship necessitate vigilance in public affairs, criticism of public officials (and corporate interests), and participation in political decision making in the interests of expanding equality of opportunity, justice, and the public good. Such activity resists the privatizing impulses of corporations, which attempt to overshadow the demands of citizenship with the demands of commerce by replacing the notion of free and equal education as a right with the notion of restricted and income-based education as a commodity venture. The challenge democratic societies face by the rise of conglomerates such as Disney—with their profound interest in shaping all facets of children's culture—can be discerned in the crisis that has emerged around the very concept of childhood and the expanding role that corporate culture plays in shaping public education. It is to this issue that I turn before taking up, more specifically, the pedagogical practices that Disney employs in its theme parks, its corporate work culture, and its school system in Celebration, Florida.

THE POLITICS OF SCHOOLING

"We need not quibble about Disney as a serious cultural phenomenon," says Peter Michelson. "We are obliged, willy-nilly, to find out what he teaches. For Disney lives. He is timeless, everywhere—the artistic extension of the Mc-Guffey Reader, and there is no keeping our children from his school."[5]

The United States appears to be in the midst of a social and cultural upheaval regarding both how it views children and how it expresses its concerns for them. Recent tragedies such as the murder of JonBenét Ramsey, the child beauty queen, and the school shootings in Jonesboro, Arkansas; Pearl, Mississippi; Paducah, Kentucky; Springfield, Oregon; and Littleton, Colorado invoke the fear that childhood innocence is being eclipsed in contemporary American society.[6] Such fears mobilize public concerns about the growing threat to children's safety and well-being. But the nation is also coping with the increasing and even convenient collapse of the boundaries between children and adults through an eager exoneration of adults, reflected in state legislation authorizing that kids as young as fourteen be prosecuted and sentenced as adults. Children are now seen as both troubled and troubling, as the mood of the country shifts from viewing children as a social investment to containing or even punishing them through expanding surveillance laws, harsher criminal codes, and the dismantling of traditional safety nets such as child welfare, health care, and school nutrition programs.

James Wagoner, the president of the social services organization Advocates for Youth, argues that the death of innocence has less to do with public concern over the fate of the nation's children than with blaming children for the very problems that society creates for them. He writes, "Young people have been portrayed almost universally as a set of problems to be managed by society: juvenile crime, teenage pregnancy, drug use. . . . That concept has taken such deep root that various institutions are permeated by it, and there's not enough of the other view, of youth as an asset, a group of people with their own perspectives on things who do pretty well."[7] The scapegoating of young people, especially those who are poor and racial minorities, points to the loss of childhood innocence, to a crisis in public discourse, and to a growing inability on the part of society to affirm and act on the principles of social justice, equity, and democratic community. As the quality of public life diminishes, not only do the most vulnerable and powerless of our population suffer, such as children, the needy, and the elderly, but also we lose, as a nation, a common vocabulary for defining and reforming those public spheres that are vital to developing and defending the meaning and experience of democratic life.

When school shooter Kipland Kinkel of Springfield, Oregon, was asked about a recent family trip to Disneyland, the youngster replied that he wanted to "punch Mickey Mouse in the nose." Although Kinkel appears to be deeply disturbed, his comment begs for a consideration of the tensions that many youth must feel about, on the one hand, the cultural iconography of Disney as a purveyor of innocence and family fun and, on the other, the harsh realities of coming of age in a society that is not only weary of its youth but also repeatedly demonstrates that kids don't count for much except as consumers. Kinkel's comment also suggests that we consider whose hunger for innocence and absolution is being satisfied by the yearly family pilgrimage of middle-class America to the Magic Kingdom.

But the discourse of innocence is not limited to the public debate about whether to invest in our children or to devise new policies to contain them; it also signifies the enormous attention that children attract from the corporate culture. Kids, especially those under fourteen years old, have become a hot item for corporations because marketeers recognize that young people "will directly spend an estimated $20 billion this year (1998), and they will influence another $200 billion. . . . [Moreover], from 1993 to 1996 alone, advertising in kid-specific media grew more than 50% to $1.5 billion, according to *Competitive Media Reporting*."[8] The debate about children's loss of innocence signifies more than society's changing attitude toward young people; it also points to the rise of a corporate culture that reasserts the primacy of individualism and competitiveness and that calls for young people to surrender their capacity to become citizens in the fullest sense— possessed of the widest range of citizen skills and rights— for a market-based notion of identity, one that suggests relinquishing their roles as critical subjects for the passive role of consuming subjects. Similarly, as corporate culture extends ever deeper into the basic institutions of civil and political society, there is a simultaneous diminishment of noncommodified public spheres such as social service centers, churches, and recreational clubs, which offer the opportunity for people to engage in dialogues and practices that address the relationship of the self to public life, our responsibility to the demands of active citizenship, and a practical politics that connects our own interests to larger public problems.[9]

As commercial culture replaces public culture and as the language of the market becomes a substitute for the language of democracy, consumerism appears to be the only kind of citizenship being offered to children.[10] Consumerism, corporatism, and technological progress become the central principles for constructing who we are and how we act. Democratic identities are replaced by consuming patterns, and the good life is constructed in terms of what we buy. In effect, the eclipse of childhood innocence can be examined critically within the broader context of the decline of democracy and the ascendance of a market culture that takes over or eliminates those public spheres crucial to the education of young people in the discourse and experience of critical citizenship. As corporate power extends its influence and reach over public schools, education is subordinated to the logic of the market and to the interests of creating corporate citizens. The commercial spheres promoting such changes include television, radio, cinema, and newspapers. They and other media are engaged in a cultural pedagogy marked by a struggle over meaning, identity, and desire. Increasingly, large corporations work to connect matters of meaning and desire to a commercial logic that constricts democratic identity and affirms the growing political and pedagogical force of culture "as a crucial site and weapon of power."[11]

Media culture has become one of the most important vehicles through which corporate executives like Michael Eisner invoke innocence in order to express their commitment to middle-class family values, the welfare of children, and their expansion into noncommercial spheres such as public schooling.[12] Such rhetoric represents more than the staged authenticity of the corporate swindle; it also works strategically to "celebrate innocence over politics and other forms of critical knowledge."[13] Corporate interest in the family also suggests the increasing recognition that youth hold the key to huge markets and profits as we move into the new millennium and that such markets can be harnessed only if the identities and desires of children can be mobilized within the vastly influential educational spheres of both popular culture and public education.

DISNEY'S CORPORATE REACH

Within the last decade, corporate power and its expansion into all aspects of everyday life has grown exponentially.[14] One of the most visible examples of such growth can be seen in the expanding role that the Walt Disney Company plays in shaping popular culture and daily life in the United States and abroad. The Disney Company is a model of the new face of corporate power at the beginning of the twenty-first century. Like many other megacorporations, its focus is on popular culture, and it continually expands its reach. Unlike Time-Warner, Westinghouse, and other large corporations, Disney is an icon of American culture and middle-class family values. It actively appeals to both parental concerns and children's fantasies as it works hard to transform every child into a lifetime consumer of Disney products and ideas. A contradiction emerges between Disney's cutthroat commercial ethos and the Disney culture, which presents itself as a paragon of virtue and childlike innocence. Disney has built its reputation on both profitability and wholesome entertainment, largely removed from issues of power, politics, and ideology. Yet this is merely the calculated rhetoric of a corporate giant, whose annual revenues in 1997 exceeded $22 billion as a result of its ability to manufacture, sell, and distribute culture on a global scale, making it the world's most powerful leisure icon.[15] Michael Ovitz, a former Disney executive, touches on the enormous power Disney wields: "Disney isn't a company as much as it is a nation-state with its own ideas and attitudes, and you have to adjust to them."[16]

The image of Disney as a political and economic power promoting a specific culture and ideology appears at odds with a public relations image that portrays the company as offering young people the promise of making their dreams come true through the pleasures of wholesome entertainment. The contradiction between the politics that shape the Disney culture and its effort to construct and influence children's culture is disturbing. But holding Disney accountable for the way it shapes children's desires and identities becomes important as the Disney corporation increasingly presents itself not only as a purveyor of entertainment and fun but also as a political force in developing models of education that influence how young people are educated in public schools, spheres traditionally understood to offer children the space for critical and intellectual development uninhibited by the relentless fascinations of consumer culture.

Some critics suggest that the Walt Disney Company is tantamount to the "evil empire."[17] And although Disney is not without its own contradictions, and although it is crucial to recognize that Disney culture is "simultaneously reactionary and progressive, nostalgic and challenging,"[18] such contradictions should be mined for the spaces of resistance they provide and for the progressive possibilities they offer. Not only are there enterprising messages and elements in many of its cultural texts (e.g., the film *Beloved*), but Disney also provides a certain measure of pleasure to the millions who buy its products, visit its theme parks, listen to its media broadcasts, and see, for example, its outstanding Broadway production of *The Lion King*.

The enormous ideological and material power that Disney exercises over civic culture raises important questions about the fate of democracy given such unbridled corporate power. Its threat to democracy is not canceled out by the fact that Disney produces a progressive television show, supports a Gay Day Festival at Disney World, and produces an avant-garde Broadway production.[19] Nor is the power of Disney to stifle dissent over the book and electronic media industries offset by the fact that varying groups, subcultures, and audiences appropriate Disney goods for their own purposes and that they do so as neither passive consumers nor dupes. These appropriations do not cancel out the systematic attempts by the Walt Disney Company, Time-Warner, Westinghouse, Philip Morris, and other market-driven industries to form powerful monopolies that wipe out competition and that exercise enormous influence over the shape and direction of children's culture—and increasingly over public life.

As part of a handful of industries that control the "country's media-cultural space,"[20] Disney represents the disturbing victory of structural power and commercial values over those competing public spheres and value systems that are critical to a just society and to democracy itself. As corporate and consumer rights prevail over citizenship rights, the tension between corporate society and civil society is either downplayed or displaced, and the commercialization of everyday life along with the waning of democratic institutions and social relations continues, though not without countervailing tendencies and organized resistance.

In what follows, I examine Disney's cultural pedagogy as it mediates between corporate culture and public culture, addressing the dominant ideologies that define the boundaries of Disney's cultural politics.

DISNEY CULTURE AND THE FALL OF THE BERLIN WALL

Michael Eisner, president of the Walt Disney Company, has suggested that the educational and political force of American entertainment is so profound that it actually undermined and, in part, was responsible for the fall of communism in Eastern Europe:

> But it may not be such an exaggeration to appreciate the role of the American entertainment industry in helping to change history. The Berlin Wall was destroyed not by the force of Western arms but by the force of Western ideas. And what was the delivery system for those ideas? It has to be admitted that to an important degree it was by American entertainment.[21]

Eisner's comments are telling because they imply a number of assumptions about Disney's own conception of entertainment and its educative force. First, Eisner acknowledges that popular culture does not merely reflect the world but actually plays a role in shaping it. Second, he admits, though indirectly, that popular culture functions as an educational force in mobilizing our interests and desires. And third, his comments imply that culture is about both ideology and power. How else could one understand or explain the conditions through which specific messages are produced, circulated, and distributed to diverse populations in vastly different parts of the globe?

After recognizing that entertainment is always an educational force, the question still remains: What is being taught? If knowledge has to first be made meaningful in its form and content in order to become critical, what revelatory messages did the American media deliver that inaugurated the fall of communism? Once again, Eisner is specific. He claims that American entertainment, with Mickey Mouse serving as its ambassador of goodwill, imparts a "diversity of individual opportunity, individual choice and individual expression, [and that] for viewers around the world, America is the place where the individual has a chance to make a better life and to have political and economic freedom."[22] This is a remarkable statement, because it presents Disney's corporate culture as synonymous with democracy itself and, in doing so, eliminates the tension between corporate values and the values of a civil society, which cannot be measured in strictly commercial terms but are critical to democracy—specifically, justice, freedom, equality, pluralism, individual rights, and rights to health care and free and equal education.

What diversity is Eisner referring to? Certainly, the ongoing attempt by Disney to turn the American landscape into a theme park for largely white, middle-class suburbanites (a week's entertainment for a family of four at Disneyland costs about $2,000, not including travel costs) does not embody the diversity that would be central to a democratic culture. When Eisner mentions individual choice and expression, he must be forgetting that the Disney corporation is run by a mere handful of people and that most corporations of its size have little to do with expanding individual choice and a great deal to do with eliminating choice. How would one explain the corporation's commitment to freedom to the 43 million Americans who have lost their jobs in the last fifteen years as a result of corporate downsizing?

Eisner celebrates freedom, but only in the discourse of

the unbridled power of the market. There is no recognition here (how could there be?) of either the limits that democracies must place on such power or the way that corporate culture and its narrow redefinition of freedom as a private good may actually present a threat to democracy equal to if not greater than that imagined under communism or any other totalitarian ideology. Benjamin Barber, responding to Eisner's comments, writes:

> How can anyone take seriously the claim that the market only gives people what they want when there is a quarter of a trillion dollar advertising industry? . . . The great myth of capitalism has been the idea that all markets do is license and legitimize choice; markets empower people to choose, to vote with their dollars, D-Marks or the yen. But, at the same time, they close down broader choices. The old example still stands: In many American cities you can choose from 25 models of automobiles, but you can't choose public transportation.[23]

DISNEY AND THE POLITICS OF INNOCENCE

Eisner does more than offer a view of Disney's ideology synonymous with American patriotism; he also reveals a central aspect of Disney culture. Disney has given new meaning to the politics of innocence as a narrative for shaping public memory and for producing a "general body of identifications"[24] that promote a sanitized version of American history. Innocence also serves as a rhetorical device that cleanses the Disney image of the messiness of commerce, ideology, and power. In other words, Disney's strategic association with childhood, a world free of contradictions and politics, not only represents the basic appeal of its theme parks and movies but also provides a model for defining corporate culture separate from the influence of corporate power. Hence, Eisner is caught in a contradiction: on the one hand, he acknowledges that corporate power uses entertainment as an educational force to shape society in its own interests. On the other hand, Eisner refuses to acknowledge responsibility for the role that Disney plays in harnessing children's identities and desires to an ever-expanding sphere of consumption; for editing public memory to reconstruct an American past in its own image; or for setting limits on democratic public life by virtue of its controlling influence on the media and its increasing presence in the schools.

Education is never innocent, because it always presupposes a particular view of citizenship, culture, and society. And yet it is this very appeal to innocence, bleached of any semblance of politics, that has become a defining feature of Disney culture and pedagogy.

The Walt Disney Company's attachment to the appeal of innocence provides a rationale for Disney both to reaffirm its commitment to children's pleasure and to downplay any critical assessments of the role Disney plays as a benevolent corporate power in sentimentalizing childhood innocence as it simultaneously commodifies it. Stripped of the historical and social constructions that give it meaning, innocence in the Disney universe becomes an atemporal, ahistorical, apolitical, and atheoretical space where children share a common bond free of the problems and conflicts of adult society. Disney markets this ideal, presenting itself as a corporate parent who safeguards this protective space for children by supplying the fantasies that nourish it.

Eisner recognizes the primacy of innocence for Disney's success, reaffirming the company's long-standing public relations position that innocence exists outside of the reach of adult society and that Disney alone provides the psychic economy through which kids can express their fantasies. He comments: "The specific appeal of Disneyland, Disney films and products—family entertainment—comes from the contagious appeal of innocence. . . . Obviously, Disney characters strike a universal chord with children, all of whom share an innocence and openness *before* they become completely molded by their respective societies."[25] Eisner's claim is important because it suggests that Disney culture reflects rather than shapes a particular version of childhood innocence and subjectivity. There is little to infer from Eisner's comments that Disney has always viewed children as an enormously productive market to fuel company profits and that old Walt Disney clearly understood the appeal to innocence as a universal mechanism for exploiting the realm of childhood fantasies in its "relentless quest for new images to sell."[26]

Old Walt may have had the best of intentions when it comes to making kids happy, but he had few doubts about the enormous commercial potential of youth. In fact, Disney was to become a pioneer not simply in marketing Disney toys but also in licensing Mickey Mouse, Snow White, and every other character turned out by the Disney imagineers to every conceivable advertising outlet. The historian Gary Cross points out that as early as the 1930s the image of Mickey Mouse appeared on "blankets, watches, toothbrushes, lamp shades, radios, breakfast bowls, alarm clocks, Christmas tree lights, ties, and clothing of all kinds."[27] Walt proved to be even more enterprising when he licensed Snow White dolls months before the release of *Snow White and the Seven Dwarfs,* the first Disney animated feature film. "No fewer than seventy corporate licenses were granted for dozens of items carrying the Snow White stamp."[28]

Michael Eisner took over the failing Walt Disney Company in 1983 and produced record revenues for the company partly by waging aggressive advertising and licensing campaigns for merchandising children's culture. Eisner established Disney as a major media outlet with the purchase of Capital Cities/ABC in 1995. One of Eisner's goals, given Disney's aggressive expansion, seems to be to make every person on the planet "a potential lifetime consumer of all things Disney, from stuffed animals to sitcoms, from Broadway musicals to three-bedroom tract homes."[29] One part innocence and three parts corporate experience seems to be the formula for the Disney magic that makes cash registers ring in 728 Disney Stores globally. The appeal of innocence seems never to have been greater, as Disney consultants such as James U. McNeal advise Eisner and his cohorts on how to tap into the $1.5 billion being spent on marketing to children. Recognizing there is "great demand by advertisers for kid media," McNeal has supported Disney's entry into children's radio through the creation of its own radio network, aptly called Radio Disney, which is aimed at children between the ages of four and twelve.[30]

Michael Eisner's rationale for Radio Disney and its intrusion into Saturday-morning children's programming is utterly predictable: "Radio Disney, our new radio network, is thriving on 13 ABC-owned radio stations across the country. By the way, I love Radio Disney. It plays on 710 AM here in Los Angeles, and I listen to it all the time. I feel a little silly because we advertise it as radio for kids. What can I do? I like the music! Maybe I need grandchildren! Breck . . . Eric . . . (Anders, you're too young) . . . do you hear that??"[31] Maybe Eisner's commentary wouldn't be subject to the charge of disingenuousness if it didn't appear in a report to Disney shareholders, a report that in its overbearing emphasis on profit margins and expansion belies Disney's attempt to appear uninterested in the bottom line. Or maybe Eisner truly believes that there is nothing wrong with making Disney culture an advertisement for America itself, a model for a corporate version of utopia aimed at creating a Disney citizenry ready and willing to purchase Disney's packaged version of history, fantasy, and the future.

In spite of his vast success in resuscitating Disney, Eisner doesn't associate himself with the image of the corporate raider but with the image of a man in touch with his inner child. It should not come as a surprise, since he has commented that running Disney "was like being left in a toy shop."[32] Alan Bryman argues that the childlike persona serves Eisner and the Disney Company well, since it "allows him to associate himself with the dream-like fantasy world and to deflect from himself a complete association with the world of business."[33] Eisner's portrayal of himself as just having fun is simply an updated version of old Walt's desire to create a world of clean, well-lighted places, a world in which adult preoccupations with complexity and moral responsibility appear out of place or, perhaps, simply irrelevant.[34]

Innocence plays a complex role in the Disney Company's attempt to market its self-image to the American public. Innocence not only registers Disney's association with a sentimentalized notion of childhood fantasy but also functions as the principal concept of moral regulation and as part of a politics of historical erasure. In Disney's moral order, innocence is "presented as the deepest truth,"[35] which when unproblematized can be used with great force and influence to legitimate the spectacle of entertainment as escapist fantasy. In addition, innocence becomes the ideological and educational vehicle through which Disney promotes conservative ideas and values as the normative and taken-for-granted "premises of a particular and historical form of social order."[36] That Disney has a political stake in creating a particular moral order favorable to its commercial interests raises questions about what it teaches in order to produce the meanings, desires, and dreams through which it attempts to subscribe all of us to the Disney worldview. In addressing this issue, I look briefly at Disney's theme parks as important pedagogical sites for rendering a version of public memory—a reading of how the past defines the present—and for articulating strategies of escapism and consumerism that reinforce an infantilized and privatized notion of citizenship.

TURNING AMERICA INTO A THEME PARK

Amid much fanfare, Disneyland opened on July 17, 1955, and became an immediate hit. By 1960 the number of visitors it attracted had grown to around 5 million annually, and by the 1990s, the number had reached an astounding 30 million a year.[37] Walt Disney set the tone for Disneyland as an embodiment of American idealism, an idealism that offered a mixture of fantasy, fun, curiosity, and optimism, on the one hand, and a strong affirmation and celebration of a mainstream view of American values and culture, on the other. Walt made this quite clear in his remarks celebrating its opening:

> The idea of Disneyland is a simple one. It will be a place for people to find happiness and knowledge. It will be a place for parents and children to share pleasant times in one another's company; a place for teachers and pupils to discover great ways of understanding and education. . . . Disneyland will be based upon and dedicated to the ideals, the dreams and the hard facts that have created America. . . . Disneyland will be something of a fair, an exhibition, a play-

ground, a community center, a museum of living facts, and a showplace of beauty and magic.[38]

A couple of years later, in an interview, Walt was even more specific, arguing that "there's an American theme behind the whole park. I believe in emphasizing the story of what made America great and what will keep it great."[39] Steven Watts summarizes how the park was organized to promote an "unproblematic celebration of the American people and their experience":

Main Street, USA, with its nostalgic images of turn-of-the-century small-town life, the heroic conquest of the West represented in Frontierland, the sturdiness of the heartland reflected in the Rivers of America, the Jungle Cruise in Adventureland with its playful pacification of the Third World, the promise of continued technological progress with Monsanto's House in the Future in Tomorrowland. The showcasing of sophisticated robot technology in the early 1960s— Audio-Animatronics, in Disney's parlance—enhanced Disneyland's celebration of the American people. The Enchanted Tiki Room, which initiated this technology in 1963, created a jovial melting-pot atmosphere as its brightly colored electronic birds comically represented French, German, Irish, and other stereotypes. But Great Moments with Mr. Lincoln was probably the culmination of the park's roboticized version of American values. In this attraction, an electronically controlled replica of the sixteenth president rose to his feet against a swelling backdrop of patriotic music and solemnly paid homage to the tradition of democratic constitutionalism in the United States.[40]

With its emphasis on safety, quality, cleanliness, and efficiency, the park provided the postwar generation an escape from the tensions of living in the atomic age. But Walt had more in mind than simply providing therapeutic relief for those anxious to flee, if only temporarily, the conflicts and traumas of modern society; he also insisted that the park provide entertainment-filled lessons that reaffirm an unqualified patriotic enthusiasm for the American way of life as experienced through the cultural matrix of sentiment, nostalgia, middle-class family values, unfettered consumerism, and the celebration of technological advancement.

Walt both built upon the success of Disneyland and amplified its possibilities with the clandestine purchase in the 1960s of more than 27,000 acres of land near Orlando, Florida, for what would eventually become Disney World. Walt had always been disturbed by the limited amount of land he had purchased for Disneyland. Purchasing land twice the size of Manhattan enabled Walt to isolate his new park from the grime and commercial incursions of the outside world. But Walt had more in mind than simply creating a theme park isolated from rivals. He wanted to control the park's environment so he could edit out the negative aspects of reality and manage both the view the public had of the outside world and the imaginative possibilities open to them once they were met by Mickey Mouse at the gates of the Magic Kingdom.[41] (In a short time, Disney World was surrounded by bars, motels, restaurants, and any number of commercial enterprises wanting to cash in on Disney's popularity, thus somewhat defeating Walt's plan.)

By the 1960s, Walt had become a staunch conservative and had developed an enormous distrust of regulatory government, a distrust matched only by his trust in American industry "and its capacity to solve social problems."[42] Disney World was envisioned to embody Walt's faith in the combined merits of entertainment, education, and corporatism. Disney World would not only be a theme park, it would also showcase the EPCOT Center (Experimental Prototype Community of Tomorrow), a utopian model of

modern urban life, a celebration of technological rational-
ity and the virtues of a corporate-designed future. EPCOT
would provide a paradigm of how corporations would solve
the problems of society through their technological wiz-
ardry: corporate culture, social engineering, and corporate
control would banish the need for politics, intellectual inquiry, and a spirited citizenship based upon democratic values and social relations. Walt was determined to build a privatized, homogeneous, and risk-free city that embodied his
version of American virtues, a city politically autonomous
and embodying a "born-again belief in the squeaky clean
virtues of front-porch USA, and nostalgia for a supposedly
uncomplicated, decent, hard-working, crime-free, rise up
and salute the flag way of life."[43]

Waving the carrot of jobs and tourist revenue, Walt secured from Florida governor Haydon Burns assurances that
the Disney World complex would be controlled almost entirely by the Disney organization. In 1967 the Florida legis-
lature conceded Disney special rights to set up the Reedy
Creek Improvement District, which not only was exempt
from many state laws but was also granted the power to
levy taxes, devise its own building codes, hire its own in-
spectors, run its own utilities, administer its own planning
and zoning laws, and maintain its own fire protection.[44] By
extracting enormous political and economic concessions
from the state of Florida, Disney World matched its relative
isolation from the outside world with a degree of governmental autonomy that allowed it to function as an independent municipality, if not a company town. Michael
Harrington commented in *Harper's Magazine* in the late
1970s that control is the key to both Disney World and the
type of future that it imagines. Disney World represented
Walt Disney's version of a corporate utopia, if not a capitalist fairy tale, embodying the dream of American business to

become "free of the pressure of democracy, [while treating] employees, customers, and children as so many pawns on the corporate board game."[45]

The ensemble of theme parks, including those opened in Tokyo and Paris in 1983 and 1992, are central to Disney's homage to white, middle-class, postwar America. The parks are a blend of "Taylorized fun," patriotic populism, and consumerism dressed up as a childhood fantasy.[46] As Steven Watts rightly argues, Disneyland in particular "can be seen as the quintessential expression of the Disney culture industry machine in the postwar era."[47] While the parks offer variations in place and purpose, they share a number of assumptions that are essential to Disney's conservative worldview. Far from representing a benign cultural force, Disney's theme parks offer prepackaged, sanitized versions of America's past, place a strong emphasis on the virtues of the individual as an essentially consuming subject, transform the work of production into the production of play, and ignore the exclusionary dynamics of class and race that permeate Disney culture.

But Disney's pedagogy has to do not only with the messages and values inscribed in the theme parks' attractions, social organization, and heritage displays but also with the manner and extent to which the ideologies that inform them are "connected to other projects in urban planning, ecological politics, product merchandising, United States domestic and global policy formation, technological innovation, and constructions of the national character."[48]

Commenting on a visit she made to Disney World in the 1990s, Elayne Rapping expressed shock on finding herself transported into a world that was totally "other" but at the same time "the most mundanely quintessential of American landscapes."[49] Being from New York City, Rapping, a cultural critic, was ill prepared to find herself in an environment entirely prepackaged and controlled. Shuffled through transportation systems with the utmost efficiency, met by an army of smiling, well-mannered cast members, and presented with an array of planned tours, she found herself in a space where "nothing could possibly go wrong because nothing could possibly happen." As a simulacrum of society, purged of conflicts, differences, and complexity, Disney World eliminates the need for the public to utilize any of those capacities that mark them as social agents. Instead, it positions them within a cultural landscape, as Rapping points out, "in which no trace of anything noncommodified, nonsimulated, nonregulated, non-smiley-faced, is visible or reachable." And yet it is precisely this editing-out of conflict, this concern with control, this overdetermined emphasis on the familiar and the uniform that appeals to the white, middle-class families that make up most of the visitors to Disney World.

Films, rides, and other Disney attractions are filled with Ozzie-and-Harriet-like images of what the family should be. Moreover, park presentations, such as the Carousel of Progress, provide the context for examining the evolution of history, technology, and the secure nature of the nuclear family within changing patterns of history and industrial development. Alan Bryman, commenting on the predominance of traditional family values in Disney's theme parks, points out that, "while waiting for the Michael Jackson science fiction rock fantasy, *Captain EO,* the assembled crowd is treated to a Kodak-sponsored series of photographs which depict the cycle of couples, babies, growing up, courtship, marriage, and back to babies. The implicit message of such presentations is clear: the conventional nuclear family is secure and will endure the vicissitudes that the future will bring to bear on it."[50]

Walt Disney and his successors recognized the importance of catering to families, but they were not interested in catering to all families. On the contrary, the appeal is to the conventional, white, middle-class, heterosexual family. Such appeals are obvious in the way in which Disney stages commodified space as a transnational shopping mall, removed from the class and ethnic diversity of real cities. Disney's theme parks function like the suburban mall, offering middle-class families an escape from crime, pollution, immigrants, the homeless, transportation problems, and work. Managed exoticism, safety, the packaged tour, and the fantasy of consumption cancel out diversity, innovation, imagination, and the uncharted excursion.

But Disney's appeal to middle-class families provides more than the familiar safety of the suburban shopping mall. It also renders history as an affirmation of a Norman Rockwell painting. Disney has also become the nostalgia machine par excellence and offers its visitors a very positive view of history, informed by what one imagineer terms "Disney realism, a sort of utopia in nature, where we carefully program out all of the negative unwanted elements and program in the positive ones."[51] This whitewashing of history—as represented in Main Street, USA, Adventureland, Frontierland, and even in the updated Tomorrowland of 1998—reaffirms a past that appeals to middle-class families, a past filled with optimism, a past that implicitly proclaims the triumph of white culture. Michael Eisner captures this sentiment: "We see Disney's America as a place where people can celebrate America, her people, struggles, victories, courage, setbacks, diversity, heroism, dynamism, pluralism, inventiveness, playfulness, compassion, righteousness, tolerance. The park [in Northern Virginia] is being designed to create interest in our rich past."[52]

Bryman suggests that the Disney parks "reinforce the 'culture of comfort' and thereby the legitimacy of the lot of

the relatively affluent middle class who are their patrons."⁵³ There are no strikes in Disneyland. No history of
labor unrest. No history of attacks on immigrants. No history of slavery or segregation. No Red scare, no McCarthy-
ism, no atom bomb.⁵⁴ Nor will one find in Disney's rewriting of public memory any mention of corporations' abuse
of labor, corporations' responsibility for acid rain, or responsibility for the effects of corporate downsizing. Not in
Disney's history. Walt Disney once announced that "Disneyland is a place where you can't get lost."⁵⁵ Disney's rewriting of public memory echoes that sentiment and offers
its patrons a history "without classes, conflict, or crime, a
world of continuous consumption, a supermarket of
fun."⁵⁶

The historian Mike Wallace uses the term "Mickey
Mouse history" to describe the merger of corporate culture
and education and the commercialization of the past. To
provide a positive environment for consumption, the Disney Company makes history safe for its audiences, with the
mythical Main Street supplying the model for many of its
attractions. Disney portrays the Gay Nineties as one of the
most optimistic periods in our history, whiting out actual
historical events. "The decades before and after the turn of
the century had their decidedly prosperous moments. But
they also included depressions, strikes on the railroads,
warfare in the minefields, squalor in the immigrant communities, lynching, imperial wars, and the emergence of
mass protests by populists and socialists. This history has
been whited out, presumably because it would have dis-
tressed and repelled visitors. As Hench noted, 'Walt wanted
to reassure people.' "⁵⁷

NOSTALGIA AND CIVIC DUTY

Disney's theme parks are the result of corporate culture's
growing awareness of the tremendous marketing potential

in the areas of family life and civic education. Its irony lost, Robert Frost's "Provide! Provide!" becomes the defining principle of responsible parenting, as consumption becomes the unifying force through which families organize themselves and their relations to others. Disney theme parks not only provide middle-class families with an upbeat version of the American past, they give such entertainment the force of civic duty. As Jane Kuenz points out, Disney's version of the past stresses that "what's important is the unity and equality we've ostensibly achieved in the marketplace, which, as we've learned in EPCOT, is synonymous with history itself."[58]

Reflecting on her trip to Disney World, Elayne Rapping deplores how the imagination is reduced to mindless routine. Encouraging spectatorship and passivity, Disney appropriates nostalgia simply to maximize consumption in the interest of fun and commerce. Main Street is developed primarily as a (disguised?) shopping mall, and attractions such as EPCOT and the World Showcase are transformed into advertisements for corporations. She notes that "memory itself is what Disney has most ambitiously and arrogantly confiscated, transformed, patented and retailed. Walk out of any of the rides or events and you're on Main Street, 1900, as Norman Rockwell would have painted it, had he been able to imagine its many varieties of mass-produced useless objects, all linked to other Disney attractions. Buy a T-shirt and be lured toward the game, or movie, or ride of the same motif."[59]

Public memory, in Disney's worldview, is inseparable from commercial culture. And this equation raises serious questions about how history is written when it is sponsored by corporate interests. As a model for a corporate notion of utopia, Disney's theme parks collapse public and historical discourse into the language of entertainment and commercialism. In the name of "edutainment," Disney imagineers clean up the abuses of history, just as they have cleaned up the mouse. The parks—in conjunction with Disney's overwhelming media presence in everything from movies, to sports, to merchandising—create audiences for advertisers. Put more succinctly, Disney educates and entertains in order to create corporate identities and to define citizens primarily as consumers and spectators. Given this goal, Disney realism raises questions regarding what the exercise of citizenship looks like within its environs. How is it possible to reconcile a critical reading of history, texts, and society with the interests of multibillion-dollar corporations such as Disney? What constitutes social agency outside of the logic of commercialism within the Disney worldview? Finally, what prevents the public from raising such questions, not to mention acting upon them?

Critics writing in the 1960s raised serious questions about Disney's cultural politics and its impact on the political and social landscape of America. Writing during the era of student demonstrations, political assassinations, and radical social reform, Richard Schickel accused Disney of fostering "unquestioning patriotism, bourgeois moral nostrums, gauche middle-class taste, racist exclusion, corporate profit mongering, [and] bland stands of social conformity."[60] If these criticisms were true in the 1960s, they would become even more apt as Disney grew more powerful under the control of Michael Eisner. Schickel and other critics underestimated the degree of economic and political power the Disney Company would wield and how it would use that power not only to continue to stripmine the imagination but also to dampen dissent and narrow the possibilities for political and cultural democracy.[61] For instance, within a few weeks after the Walt Disney Company acquired ABC, it issued a formal apology to Philip Morris—a major TV advertiser through Kraft foods—and paid millions of dollars to cover the bills of tobacco company lawyers. The tobacco company had initiated a suit against ABC before the Disney takeover in response to a program broadcast of *Day One,* documenting how Philip Morris attempted to "control levels of nicotine" in its cigarettes. In light of the apology and settlement, the *New York Times* "reported that the lawsuit was part of a new tobacco industry strategy aimed at influencing news coverage."[62]

If there were ever any doubts about Disney's linkage of corporate power with the stifling of dissent, such doubts are disappearing. After taking over ABC, the Walt Disney Company fired the popular, progressive talk-show host Jim Hightower, after he remarked on his show that he now "worked for a rodent." Lacking neither popular backing nor advertising revenue, Hightower was sacked because he denounced the Disney takeover of ABC and the recent passage of the Telecommunications Act, which opened the door for media mergers and buyouts.[63] Disney's rigid corporate policy has also led to the discontinuation of Insane Clown Posse's hip-hop schlock album, *The Great Milenko,* initially distributed through Hollywood Records, now owned by Disney. More recently, ABC News president David Westin decided to kill a proposed *20/20* television piece based on Peter and Rochelle Schweizer's book, *Disney: The Mouse Betrayed,* a scorching right-wing critique of ABC's owner, the Walt Disney Company. The implications of such actions are clear: investigative reporters and the news division cannot do stories critical of their boss, the Walt Disney Company. As one veteran ABC correspondent, speaking on the condition of anonymity, stated in the *Philadelphia Inquirer*: "The nightmare is that the news division and our ability to be reporters would appear to be compromised because of our ownership."[64]

The force of such power does more than shut down dissent and suppress distasteful facts about the Disney Company. Disney has also raised the stakes on controlling foreign markets for its cultural goods. As a major producer and distributor of films, Disney plays a significant role in wiping out local film productions and distribution. It is bad enough that American films already have 90 percent of the German market, 65 percent of the French market, 85 percent of the Italian market, and nearly all of the British market.[65] One indication of Disney's greed can be seen in its policy for distributing and packaging its theater productions:

> In the case of *The Lion King,* Disney has chosen to change the very rules by which the theatrical game is played. For producers who want to showcase *The Lion King* in other parts of the world, the rights are available only if they accept a package deal of five more productions. While packaging is common in the film industry, it is a rarity in theater, when even a hit show can operate in the red for years. Disney's extravagant productions thus far suggest that even one flop could sink a producer who accepts the deal. It's hardly surprising that there are grumblings of dissent among the rave reviews.[66]

Surprisingly, the Walt Disney Company's rapid and aggressive expansion, coupled with its willingness to stifle dissent within its ranks and competition from the outside, has not undercut its self-proclaimed image as the "happiest place on earth." On the contrary, it is a place in which corporate dreams and versions of history are manufactured to catchy dance tunes, glitzy movies, lifelike robots, and "the latest in special effects."[67] Or, as the *Nation* points out, the Walt Disney Company is part of a "national entertainment state," for which issues of power and control loom large in its worldview.[68] The values that inform the Disney culture become more clear when analyzing the pedagogical practices it uses to initiate its employees into Disney's version of corporate citizenship.

WORKING FOR A RODENT

> Why should I run for mayor [of Los Angeles] when I'm already king?
>
> —Walt Disney

Disney's corporate culture and the values that underlie its moral and political order are evident in the training programs the company provides for its employees, especially the programs incorporated into the curriculum at Walt Disney University in California and Disney University in Florida. Control, efficiency, predictability, and uniformity are the hallmarks of Disney's approach to people management, a style so successful that it is now marketed to other companies in an intensive three-day seminar. According to one seminar manager:

> The formula for pixie dust is simple: Training + Communication + Care = Pride. By carefully training and developing cast members, by making all cast communications timely and effective, and by encouraging a friendly and caring work environment, Disney creates a strong sense of pride in each cast member, which in turn inspires him or her to give first-rate service to all Disney guests. The participants in the people management seminar learn first-hand how the pixie-dust formula is applied to all aspects of the Disney World operation.[69]

Work culture in Disney is subject to the same control that permeates all other aspects of its organization. Fantasy mediates and subordinates issues of power, politics, and ethics in the Disney work culture through the intervention of what can be called Disney discourse. As a customer is transformed into a "guest," an employee becomes a "host" or "hostess" or a "cast member." Hiring for a job becomes "casting," a uniform magically changes into a "costume," an accident is reduced to an "incident," and so it goes. Because the Disney organization considers itself a family, all cast members are on a first-name basis. Michael Eisner is "Michael."[70] But however lighthearted and fanciful it might seem, Disney discourse does not displace the rigid and authoritarian nature of the workplace.

"Casting" for new employees follows very strict rules, as I found out when a friend of mine working in the Career and Life Education Office in a Pennsylvania college received a memo from the Disney Company. It stipulated the guidelines that students at the college were to follow in order to attend Disney's on-campus "informational session." It seems that Disney wanted a particular type of student to attend, as indicated in the detailed dress codes it provided for both men and women. The men were to wear a suit with a color-coordinated shirt; the suit fabric was to be one "traditionally accepted for business." No necklaces, bracelets, or earrings were allowed, nor were male students permitted to have a mustache, beard, or hair "beyond or covering any part of the ears." No one was to show up with an "extreme look, including shaving the head or eyebrows." And, of course, no one would be admitted who had visible tattoos. Women were to wear a suit, a dress, or a pants outfit (no jumpsuits, T-shirts, sleeveless dresses or blouses, and no clinging fabrics or suede leather). No more than two necklaces could be worn, and these were not to exceed thirty inches in length. And in case these young women missed the point, they were not to wear more than one ring per hand.

There is more going on here than an old-fashioned prud-
ishness. There is a measure of control that is excessively
regulating and authoritarian. Furthermore, Disney's selective hiring practices appear consistent with its homogeneous, sanitized theme parks: each facet of the Disney experience is aimed at reassuring "guests," who increasingly
experience the desire for social and spatial isolation, that
they will not have to deal with difference.

Disney's theme parks are designed, in part, to erase problems associated with low-skill, low-paying, and routinized
labor. Happy faces are a mandatory part of "the costume"
for "cast members" at Disney. The reality of work has been
excised both from the Disney discourse and from the public's view. As if modeled after the Aldous Huxley novel
Brave New World, the dystopian world of work is banished.
Utilities, power lines, storage pipes, workers' quarters, employee transportation, and all other signs of a labor force
are relegated to a vast subterranean network of corridors
and tunnels. The Seven Dwarfs' tune "Whistle While You
Work" takes on surreal overtones as the link between leisure and labor is separated from view in the parks. Moreover, by undermining the reality of labor, the Walt Disney
Company eliminates labor's resistance to Disney's social
engineering and heavy-handed discipline. Citizenship in
Disney's world means more than acquiring specific job
skills; it means, as one employee puts it, learning "a new
way of life: the Disney Way."[71] Dick Nunis, vice president
in charge of Disney theme parks, puts it more bluntly.
"When we hire a girl [as a hostess], we point out that we're
not hiring her for a job, but casting her for a role in our
show. And we give her a costume and a philosophy to go
with it."[72]

The Disney philosophy preaches everything from employee demeanor (smile, use courteous phrases, and don't

be stuffy) to how to dress, how to use Disney language, and how to embrace Disney culture. Pedagogically, employees are drawn into a strong corporate culture through classroom training that emphasizes memorizing elaborate checklists of appearance standards. New employees are given written quizzes on Disney rules. One pedagogical strategy includes exposing workers to an endless chant of inane Disney mottos such as "We work while others play!" "We never say no because we know the answers." And "We smile that extra mile."[73] Disney's emphasis on learning rules and mottos is matched also by attempts to influence its employees' emotional responses. As John Van Maanen, a former Disney worker, explains, "Employees are told repeatedly that if they are happy and cheerful at work, so, too, will the guests at play. Inspirational films, hearty pep talks, family imagery, and exemplars of corporate performance are all representative of the strong symbolic stuff of these training rites." Disney even provides its employees with a definition of Disney corporate culture to memorize, allegedly to help give them an emotional lift as they begin their workday: "Dis-ney Cor-po-rate Cul-ture (diz'ne kor'-pr'it kul'cher) n 1. Of or pertaining to the Disney organization, as a: philosophy underlying all business decisions; b: the commitment of top leadership and management to that philosophy; c: the actions taken by individual cast members that reinforce that image."[74]

Disney's pedagogy for employees is characterized by a number of features, but several stand out. First, Disney's training programs bestow "identity through a process carefully set up to strip away the job relevance of other sources of identity and learned response and to replace them with others of organizational relevance."[75] Second, there is little room for individuality and experimentation by employees. Every behavior and action, from how one dresses to how one responds to questions raised by guests, are scripted by someone in authority. Innovation is viewed as a breach of policy, and nonconformity is swiftly eliminated from Disney's technocratic utopia. For instance, it was recently reported that "when skippers on Disneyland's famous Jungle Cruise updated their standard shtick with mild jokes about Los Angeles and Rush Limbaugh, they were summarily dismissed despite positive guest reaction."[76]

Third, Disneyland employees work in a rigid pecking order: supervisors and foremen function less to offer advice and guidance than to monitor underlings in case they break a rule. In his study of Disney work culture in the early 1990s, Van Maanen says that "supervisors in Tomorrowland are . . . famous for . . . hiding in the bushes above the submarine caves, timing the arrivals and departures of the supposedly fully loaded boats making the $8^1/2$ minute cruise under the polar icecaps. . . . In short, supervisors . . . are regarded by ride operators as sneaks and tricksters out to get them and representative of the dark side of park life."[77] Finally, in a culture governed by such strict disciplinary procedures, it is not surprising that firings are a frequent occasion at the theme parks. These features fly in the face of Disney's familial rhetoric. Moreover, such rhetoric is at odds with a hierarchy in the Disney work culture marked by enormous inequalities in power, income, and prestige. In fact, Van Maanen reports that while working at Disneyland he was warned about growing hair over his ears. He did not anticipate, however, the form his eventual dismissal was to take:

> Dismissal began by being pulled off the ride after my work shift had begun by an area supervisor in full view of my cohorts. A forced march to the administration building followed, where my employee card was turned over and a

short statement read to me by a personnel officer as to the formal cause of my termination. Security officers then walked me to the employee locker room where my work uniforms and equipment were collected and my personal belongings returned to me while an inspection of my locker was made. The next stop was the time shed, where my employee's time card was removed from its slot, marked "terminated" across the top in red ink, and replaced in its customary position (presumably for Disneylanders to see when clocking on or off the job over the next few days). As now an ex-rider operator, I was escorted to the parking lot, where two security officers scraped off the employee parking sticker attached to my car. All these little steps of status degradation in the Magic Kingdom were quite public.[78]

Van Maanen's experience raises serious questions about Disney's pedagogical practices. Disney's reaction in this case appears excessive, given the sacrifices that the organization demands of its employees—unquestioned obedience, scripted responses, craven servility—coupled with the fact that most of its jobs are low paying.

The profound routinization of work at Disney theme parks is matched only by the profound routinization of leisure and amusement in these parks. Both work and pleasure signify apathy, intellectual laziness, and subservience. What Disney offers is not "flight from a wretched reality but from the last remaining thought of resistance."[79] What counts as knowledge and citizenship within the pedagogies at work in the Disney culture undermine any viable notion of critical agency, independent thought, and social responsibility. Disney "cast members" often find themselves working within a mythical discourse that appears to undermine their ability to confront the harsh realities that visitors sometimes have to face in the Disney theme parks. Disney's strict rules regarding how accidents are dealt with appear to be at odds with Disney's commitment to ensuring the health and safety of both its employees and its theme park visitors. Accidents are labeled incidents, people are transported to hospitals in low-profile vehicles rather than in ambulances so as not to rupture Disney's claim to being the "happiest place on earth," and when serious injuries do occur there appears to be a systematic attempt on the part of the Disney corporation to protect its corporate image rather than respond in a publicly responsible manner. For example, Lisa Stern, a lawyer in litigation with Disney, claims that since the opening of the Indiana Jones Adventure Ride on March 3, 1995, over 100 people have been injured from the ride, including a Disney manager who suffered a disc injury in her back.[80] Many people have written letters complaining about the ride, and in one case, Zipora Jacob, a forty-four-year-old mother of two, claims that after she got off the Indiana Jones Adventure Ride in 1992 she vomited and collapsed. According to her suit claim, she eventually fell into a coma and suffered severe brain damage, including a tear in her brain, which has required four major operations to repair.[81] What is disturbing about this case is what Disney's response has been to it. Disney not only did little to respond to a number of complaints about the ride or resulting injuries, but, according to Barry Novack, a lawyer representing Zipora Jacob, Disney "continually stalled the discovery process by refusing to produce documents regarding injury claims and safety related to the Indiana Jones ride."[82] Moreover, Disney tried to dismiss the Jacob lawsuit by claiming that a "head injury" is part of the "inherent risk" a Disney theme park visitor must assume on such a ride. Of course, Disney does not mention that the ride may have been unsafe, or that brain damage may be a high-risk trade-off for a theme park ride. In a brief to the

Superior Court of the State of California for the county of Los Angeles, Novack argues:

> Despite the fact that Disney employees and guests were being injured on the ride, the Disney defendants kept the ride at its injury-causing level and failed to heed the warnings of its injured guests. The Disney defendants acted in conscious disregard of the public safety by not adequately testing the ride before it was opened to the public and in keeping the ride at its injury-causing levels as of the time Zipora was injured.[83]

Disney has tried to dismiss the case, arguing that Jacob knowingly exposed herself to the possibility of a brain hemorrhage on the grounds she knew about the dangers inherent in the ride. Disney also tried to dismiss a judge from the case, claiming he was prejudiced against the interests of Disney. There is nothing innocent about Disney when it comes to protecting its profits and its corporate image.

*   *   *

The most important form of education fosters self-reflection and public responsibility, two qualities that, in the Disney ideology, are secular sacrilege. The "naturalized" world of Disney, with its squeaky-clean image, false happiness, and cartoonish social imagery exacts a high price both politically and ethically.

Theodor Adorno, writing about education after Auschwitz, raises a clarion call against pedagogies—such as those fostered by the Walt Disney Company—that destroy "the particular and the individual together with their power of resistance. With the loss of their identity and power of resistance, people also forfeit those qualities by virtue of which they are able to pit themselves against what at some moment might lure them again to commit atrocity."[84] While I do not suggest that Disney's pedagogy has a direct link to the atrocities committed at Auschwitz, I do suggest that, in analyzing Disney's corporate pedagogy, we need to ask whether such practices reproduce the conditions of a barbarous past.

Disney's educational practices should be understood as part of a broader assault on public discourse, which dispenses with the principles of autonomy, critical self-reflection, and self-determination. Disney's pedagogy is not about the power of the imagination to recognize the benefit and limitations of reality in order to enter into critical dialogue with it and transform it when necessary. On the contrary, Disney offers a fantasy world grounded in a promotional culture and bought at the expense of citizens' sense of agency and resistance, as the past is purged of its subversive elements and translated into a nostalgic celebration of entrepreneurship and technological progress. Fantasy, as a Disney trademark, has no language for imagining public life and, as such, cannot be self-critical about its own relationship to it. It is within the context of Disney's corporate pedagogy that I analyze, in the next chapter, the Walt Disney Company's development of its new town, Celebration, and its move into public schooling.

NOTES

1. Michael Eisner, "Planetized Entertainment," *New Perspectives Quarterly* 12:4 (1995), p. 8.

2. Michael D. Eisner, "Letter to Shareholders," *The Walt Disney Company 1997 Annual Report* (Burbank, Calif.: Walt Disney Company, 1997), p. 3.

3. Stuart Hall, "The Centrality of Culture: Notes on the Cultural Revolutions of Our Time," in Kenneth Thompson, ed., *Media and Cultural Regulation* (Thousand Oaks, Calif.: Sage, 1997), p. 209.

4. For an excellent analysis of the relationship between education and social justice, see R. W. Connell, *Schools and Social Justice* (Philadelphia: Temple University Press, 1993).

5. Peter Michelson, "What Disney Teaches," *New Republic,* July 6, 1968, p. 31.

6. See, for instance, Peter Applebome, "No Room for Children in a World of Little Adults," *New York Times,* May 10, 1998, p. 1.

7. Ann Powers, "Who Are These People, Anyway?" *New York Times,* April 29, 1998, p. E1, 8. For a brilliant attack on the scapegoating of young people, see Mike Males, Framing Youth: Ten Myths About the Next Generation (Monroe, ME: Common Courage Press, 1999).

8. "Hey Kid, Buy This!" *Business Week,* June 30, 1997, p. 64.

9. See Harry C. Boyte, "Citizenship Education and the Public World," *Civic Arts Review* (Fall 1992), pp. 4–9.

10. This point is addressed in Powers, "Who Are These People, Anyway?"

11. Lawrence Grossberg, "Toward a Genealogy of the State of Cultural Studies," in Cary Nelson and Dilip Parameshwar Gaonkar, eds., *Disciplinarity and Dissent in Cultural Studies* (New York: Routledge, 1996), p. 142.

12. In his recent autobiography, Eisner presents himself as the ideal chief executive of a family-oriented company while conveniently leaving out old Walt's anti-Semitism, his red-baiting of Disney cartoonists in order to break their union, or the firing of the popular progressive talk-radio host Jim Hightower once Disney bought Cap Cities. See Michael Eisner with Tony Schwartz, *Work in Progress* (New York: Random House, 1998). Geraldine Fabrikant, in a review of the book, captures the flavor of Eisner's self-serving discourse. She writes: "The autobiography of Michael D. Eisner, the Chairman of Walt Disney, is a true Disney production: a PG-rated adventure with broad family appeal where the hero, by dint of hard work, sound judgment and—yes— brilliance, triumphs over adversity. It's 'The Lion King' in corporate America." Geraldine Fabrikant, "Top Mouse," *New York Times Book Review,* November 8, 1998, p. 28.

13. Chris Rojek, "Disney Culture," *Leisure Studies* 12 (1993), p. 133.

14. Two recent critical commentaries are Robert W. McChesney, *Corporate Media and the Threat to Democracy* (New York: Seven Stories Press, 1997); Erik Barnouw et al., *Conglomerates and the Media* (New York: New Press, 1997).

15. Figures are from Eisner, "Letter to Shareholders," p. 2.

16. Peter Bart, "Disney's Ovitz Problem Raises Issues for Showbiz Giants," *Daily Variety,* December 16, 1996, p. 1.

17. See, for instance, Ariel Dorfman and Armand Mattelart, *How to Read Donald Duck* (New York: International General, 1975); Matt Roth, "A Short History of Disney-Fascism," *Jump Cut* 40 (1996), pp. 15–20; and Carl Hiassen, *Team Rodent: How Disney Devours the World* (New York: Ballantine, 1998); Peter Schweizer and Rochelle Schweizer, *Disney: The Mouse Betrayed: Greed, Corruption, and Children at Risk* (Washington, D.C.: Regnery, 1998).

18. Scott Bukatman, "There's Always Tomorrowland: Disney and the Hypercinematic Experience," *October* 15 (1991), p. 58.

19. For an excellent critique of Disney's alleged progressive policies toward gays and lesbians, see Stuart Gill, "Never-Never Land," *Out* (March 1998), pp. 70–113.

20. For an excellent commentary on this issue, see Herbert I. Schiller, "Corporate Sponsorship," *Art Journal* (Fall 1991), pp. 56–59.

21. Eisner, "Planetized Entertainment," p. 9.

22. Ibid.

23. Benjamin Barber, "The Making of McWorld," *New Perspectives Quarterly* 12:4 (1995), p. 16.

24. Kenneth Burke, *A Rhetoric of Motives* (Berkeley: University of California Press, 1962), p. 26.

25. Eisner, "Planetized Entertainment." Italics mine.

26. Mike Wallace, *Mickey Mouse History* (Philadelphia: Temple University Press, 1996), p. 170.

27. Gary Cross, *Kid's Stuff: Toys and the Changing World of American Childhood* (Cambridge: Harvard University Press, 1997), p. 105.

28. Ernest Larsen, "Compulsory Play," *Nation,* March 16, 1998, p. 32.

29. Hiassen, *Team Rodent,* pp. 6–7.

30. Andrea Adelson, "Children's Radio Pioneer Is Challenged by Disney," *New York Times,* July 21, 1997, p. D10.

31. Eisner, "Letter to Shareholders," p. 5.

32. Alan Bryman, *Disney and His Worlds* (New York: Routledge, 1995), p. 57.

33. Ibid.

34. For a concise yet devastating critique of what Eisner leaves out of his rendering of Disney history, see Mark Crispin Miller, "Michael Eisner, Launderer Extraordinaire," in *Slate* (electronic journal), posted October 14, 1998, on <www.slate.com/Code/BookClub/BookClub.asp?show = 10/14/98>.

35. Chris Rojek, "Disney Culture," *Leisure Studies* 12 (1993), p. 121.

36. Philip Corrigan and Derek Sayer, *The Great Arch* (London: Basil Blackwell, 1985), p. 4.

37. Figures are from Steven Watts, *The Magic Kingdom: Walt Disney and the American Way of Life* (New York: Houghton Mifflin, 1998), p. 387; and Michael Billing, "Sod Baudrillard! Or Ideology in Disney World," in Herbert Simons and Michael Billing, eds., *After Postmodernism* (Thousand Oaks, Calif.: Sage, 1994), p. 150.

38. Leonard Mosley, *Disney's World: A Biography* (New York: Stein and Day, 1985), p. 221.

39. Both quotations are from Watts, *Magic Kingdom* pp. 392, 393.

40. Ibid.

41. On the issue of control in the parks, see Michael Sorkin, "See You in Disneyland," in Sorkin, ed., *Variations on a Theme Park* (New York: Noonday, 1992), pp. 205–32.

42. Watts, *Magic Kingdom,* p. 441.

43. Stephen F. Mills, "Disney and the Promotion of Synthetic Worlds," *American Studies International* 28:2 (1990), p. 73.

44. Hiassen, *Team Rodent,* p. 27.

45. Michael Harrington, "To the Disney Station," *Harper's* 258 (Jan. 1979), p. 39.

46. The term "Taylorized fun" is taken from Sorkin, "See You in Disneyland," p. 223.

47. Watts, *Magic Kingdom*, p. 391.

48. Eric Smoodin, "How to Read Walt Disney," in Smoodin, ed., *Disney Discourse: Producing the Magic Kingdom* (New York: Routledge, 1994), pp. 4–5.

49. Elayne Rapping, "A Bad Ride at Disney World," *Progressive* (November 1995), p. 36.

50. Bryman, *Disney and His Worlds*, pp. 87–88.

51. Wallace, *Mickey Mouse History*, pp. 136–37.

52. Michael D. Eisner, "Critics of Disney's America on the Wrong Track," *USA Today*, July 12, 1994, p. 10A.

53. Bryman, *Disney and His Worlds*, p. 141.

54. A great deal of material points to Disney's omissions in constructing history; see, for example, Stephen Fjellman, *Vinyl Leaves* (Boulder, Colo.: Westview, 1992); Rojek, "Disney Culture"; Jon Wiener, "Tall Tales and True," *Nation*, January 31, 1994, pp. 133–35; Wallace, *Mickey Mouse History;* Bryman, *Disney and His Worlds*.

55. Bukatman, "There's Always Tomorrowland," p. 56.

56. Wallace, *Mickey Mouse History*, p. 138.

57. Ibid., p. 137.

58. Jane Kuenz, "It's a Small World After All: Disney and the Pleasures of Identification," *South Atlantic Quarterly* 92:1 (1993), p. 78.

59. Rapping, "A Bad Ride at Disney World," p. 37.

60. See Watts, *Magic Kingdom*, p. 471; Schickel's own book is an important critique of Disney. Richard Schickel, *The Disney Version* (New York: Simon and Schuster, 1985, originally published in 1968).

61. See, for example, Jon Wiener's tale of how Disney has attempted to censor books dealing with the legacy of Walt Disney and the chilling effect such pressure has had on authors who refuse to grant the Walt Disney Company such power. Wiener, "Murdered Ink," *Nation*, May 31, 1993, pp. 743–50.

62. Jeff Cohen and Norman Solomon, "In Disneyland, Jour-

nalism Means Saying You're Sorry," *Extra!* (November/December 1995), p. 20.

63. Norman Solomon, "Three Men and a Mouse," *Z Magazine* (January 1998), pp. 63–64.

64. See Gail Shister, "Decision to Kill '20/20' piece on Disney Upsets ABC News Staffers," *Philadelphia Inquirer,* October 15, 1998, p. D6.

65. Figures are from Costa-Gavras, "Resisting the Colonels of Disney," *New Perspectives Quarterly* 12:4 (1995), p. 6.

66. Liane Bonin, "The Tragic Kingdom," *Detour Magazine* (April 1998), p. 71.

67. Wallace, *Mickey Mouse History,* p. 134.

68. Mark Crispin Miller and Janine Jacquet Biden, "The National Entertainment State," *Nation,* June 3, 1996, pp. 23–26.

69. Paul L. Blocklyn, "Making Magic: The Disney Approach to People Management," *Personnel* 65:12 (1989), p. 29. For an inside look at Disney's work culture, see David Koenig, *Mouse Tales: A Behind-The-Ears Look at Disneyland* (New York: Bonaventure Press, 1995).

70. Ibid., p. 32.

71. Alison Gardy, "They're Doing It for Mickey," *California Magazine* 14:1 (1989), p. 23.

72. Bryman, *Disney and His Worlds,* p. 108.

73. Gardy, "They're Doing It for Mickey," p. 24.

74. John Van Maanen, "The Smile Factory: Work at Disneyland," in Peter J. Frost, Larry F. Moore, Meryl Reis Louis, Craig C. Lundberg, and Joanne Martin, eds., *Reframing Organizational Culture* (Newbury Park, Calif.: Sage, 1991), pp. 67, 65.

75. Ibid., p. 73.

76. Bonin, "The Tragic Kingdom."

77. Van Maanen, "The Smile Factory," p. 69.

78. Ibid., p. 76.

79. Theodor Adorno and Max Horkheimer, *Dialectic of the Enlightenment* (New York: Herder and Herder, 1972, originally published in 1944), p. 144.

80. For a specific reference to the court case in which docu-

mentation was produced indicating that hundreds of people have been injured on the Indiana Jones ride, along with claims of a Disney cover-up, see Denise Levin, "It's a Dangerous, Litigious World, Disney Suit Says," *Los Angeles Daily Journal*, January 7, 1999, pp. 1, 8. See also Stuart Pfeiffer, "Trial Nears Over Alleged Wild Disney Ride," *Orange County Register*, December 30, 1998, pp. 1–2; see also Elaine Gale, "Lawsuit Blames Injuries on Park Ride," *Los Angeles Times* December 10, 1998, pp. 1–2.

81. Cited in Stuart Pfeiffer, "Trial Nears Over Alleged Wild Disney Ride"; see also Gale, "Lawsuit Blames Injuries on Park Ride."

82. Levin, "It's a Dangerous, Litigious World, Disney Suit Says," p. 1.

83. Zipora Jacob, et al., Plaintiff v. The Walt Disney Company, et al., Defendants, Case No. BC 153319, Superior Court of the State of California for the County of Los Angeles, December 9, 1998. Filed by Barry Novack, Attorney for the Plaintiff, November 25, 1998, p. 5.

84. Theodor W. Adorno, *Critical Models: Interventions and Catchwords,* translated by Henry W. Pickford (New York: Columbia University Press, 1998), p. 193.

2

LEARNING WITH DISNEY

It is time to recognize that the true tutors of our children are not schoolteachers or university professors but filmmakers, advertising executives and pop culture purveyors. Disney does more than Duke, Spielberg outweighs Stanford, MTV trumps MIT. It is not from their schools that children learn to obsess over the President's private sexual conduct.

—Benjamin R. Barber, the *Nation*

Public education has become one of the most contested public spheres in political life at the turn of the twenty-first century. More than any other institution, public schools serve as a reminder of both the promise and the shortcomings of the social, political, and economic forces that shape society. Public schools provide a critical referent for measuring the degree to which American society fulfills its obligation to provide all students with the knowledge and skills necessary for critical citizenship and the possibilities of democratic public life. Embodying the contradictions of the larger society, schools offer both a challenge and a threat to attempts by conservatives and liberals alike to remove the language of critique from the discourse of democracy and to diminish citizenship to a largely privatized affair, in which civic responsibilities are reduced to the act of consuming. No longer institutions designed to benefit all members of the community, public schools, along with other public goods, are refashioned in market terms designed to serve the narrow interests of individual consumers and national economic policies.

Diminishing the role that schools might play as democratic public spheres, corporate culture has redefined the meaning and purpose of schooling in accordance with the interests of global capitalism. As governmental support for public schools dries up, corporations attempt to harness all educational institutions to corporate control through calls for privatization, vouchers, so-called choice programs, and diverse forms of school–business partnerships. Rewriting the tradition of schooling as a public good, corporations abstract questions of equity from excellence and subsume the social and political mission of schooling within the ideology and logic of the market. In this scenario, public education is replaced by the call for privately funded educational institutions or for school–business partnerships that can ignore civil rights, exclude students who are class and racially disenfranchised, and blur the lines between religion and the state.

The current assault against public schooling is part of a broader project to dismantle all public spheres that refuse to be strictly governed by the instrumental logic of the market. As such, the battle waged over education must be understood, more generally, as a battle for deepening and expanding democratic public life. Such a struggle suggests that all public goods not be surrendered to the market and that the political function of culture be linked to creating citizens who can challenge established conventions and reflect critically on pressing social and economic problems.

More and more, the absolutely crucial political and peda-gogical questions to raise in the age of the "national enter-tainment state"[1] should be, Who controls the production of culture? Who has access to the meanings produced by media monopolies? And whose interests do these mean-ings serve? What does it mean to make culture more than entertainment, spectacle, consumption, and tourism?

We can discover how democratic societies reassert the primacy of a nondogmatic, progressive politics by analyz-ing how culture as a force for resistance is related to power, education, and agency. Such an analysis suggests the need to understand how culture shapes our everyday lives. Cul-ture constitutes a defining principle in the struggle over meaning, identity, social practices, and institutional ma-chineries of power, a struggle that can be waged by insert-ing the pedagogical into the political and by expanding the meaning of the pedagogical by recognizing the "educa-tional force of our whole social and cultural experience [as one] that actively and profoundly teaches."[2] Clearly, for such a pedagogical project to take root, the corporate en-croachment into public and higher education needs to be challenged vigorously. I address this issue, in part, by ana-lyzing the implications of the recent corporate expansion of Disney into public schooling through its development of a business–school partnership with the Celebration School in Florida.

MICKEY GOES TO SCHOOL

Walt Disney once said, "I'd love to be part of building a school of tomorrow. . . . This might be a pilot operation for the teaching age—to go out across the country and across the world."[3] This desire has been realized in several ways,

as the Walt Disney Company has a long history of involvement in public and higher education through partnerships, internships, and nontraditional programs. College students can spend up to ten weeks in Disneyland or Disney World attending seminars to learn about the leisure and entertainment industries. They also get on-site, hands-on experience in such areas as engineering, marketing, and animation. A program called College Plus invites more than 450 college students a year from California colleges to work and study at Disneyland.[4]

The Challenge Program in Florida is designed to offer potential dropouts the opportunity to attend school at Disney World for four hours in the morning and work at the park in the afternoon. Disney also has a partnership with the Monterey High School in Burbank, California, in which cast members from the Disney Studios in Burbank teach classes throughout the academic year. Disney also sends its cast members to high schools and colleges to discuss with students what it is like to work for Disney and how their own education relates to the world of work. Disney's involvement in these programs appears to be a mix of public service and self-interest, with the latter dominating. Disney's educational efforts are largely judged by how they affect the "organization's future labor pool." As one Disney supervisor put it, "We want the students [we hire] to be as skillful as possible."[5]

As important as these educational ventures are, they do not give Disney high visibility for its educational efforts, nor do they provide a public relations opportunity to focus Disney's role nationally in education. As far back as 1993, the Disney Company entered into negotiations with Chris Whittle to buy a controlling stake in the Edison Project and Channel One, both for-profit educational ventures. The deal fell through. And once Disney decided to build a new town, Celebration, it altered its plans to build a for-profit school system and entered into a partnership with Osceola County School District and Stetson University in Florida to develop a model school. But before taking up Disney's attempt to build "the school of the future," it is necessary to make some brief remarks about the context for such a school, the town of Celebration.

Disney's involvement with public schooling took a dramatic turn in the last few years when Michael Eisner and the Disney Company decided to build America's ideal community with the development of a brand-new town named Celebration, located just a few miles south of the Magic Kingdom, near Disney World in Orlando. A carefully marketed version of a small town, and a response to Disney's "perceived lack of community in American life,"[6] Celebration is a reaffirmation of the current assumption that only a corporate-driven culture "can address the problems of the city with creativity and efficiency."[7] According to Eisner, "We looked at what made communities great in our past, added what we've learned from the best practices of today, and combined that with a vision and hope for strong communities in the future."[8] Of course, Eisner also looked to the booming securities industries, capitalizing on the paranoid demands of the white middle class, whose image of the city is characterized by street violence, drug trafficking, racial and ethnic tensions, homelessness, and joblessness. This class, lacking firsthand knowledge of inner-city conditions, seizes upon the residential enclave or the restricted, if not fortified, suburb as a sanctuary. "Security" in this sense has "less to do with personal safety than with the degree of personal insulation in resident, work, consumption and travel environments, from 'unsavory' groups and individuals, even crowds in general."[9]

In Celebration, pedestrian-friendly streets are lined by

houses that occupy tiny lots offering inhabitants a proxim-
ity to each other that fosters visibility, conversation, and
the pleasures of small-town life. Diversity is an architec-
tural matter, the houses ranging from moderately expensive to extremely costly. Diversity does not, however, extend to the poor; and most of the inhabitants of
Celebration are white.[10] When it came to imagining the future, Disney took a lesson from the original Walt and from
the Disney imagineers and envisioned the future in corporate and technological terms. Each house is hooked up to
the dreams embodied in the information superhighway by
a fiber-optic cable system linked to television, telephone,
and computer systems. Residents with personal computers
have access to an "intranet" service, which allows them to
communicate with each other through electronic chat
rooms and to have access to community news.

But Celebration is more than a marriage between Norman Rockwell and Bill Gates: it also mirrors Disney's obsession with control. Living in Celebration has a price. Safety
and security are exchanged for a significant loss of control
over a number of decisions that homeowners make in most
other communities. Much of Celebration, from its architecture to its horticulture, is scripted by the folks at Disney.
Nobody can get lost in Celebration. The rules include not
being allowed to hang the wash out to dry, keeping the
grass cut, not being able to live elsewhere for more than
three months at a time, holding only one garage sale in any
twelve-month period, displaying only white or off-white
window coverings, and using only approved house paint
colors. Big Brother in the nineties doesn't just come in the
form of a totalitarian state, it also comes with a smiley face,
masking the watchful eye of privatized government. When
New York Times reporter Michael Pollan asked one Disney
master planner about the excessive restrictions, he re-

sponded, "Regimentation can release you."[11] Pollan's revelations aptly capture the middle-class fear of freedom that feeds the growing hatred of cities and the risks associated with genuinely democratic public space and integrated social relations.

According to Bob Shinn, a senior vice president of Walt Disney Imagineering, Celebration is aimed at fulfilling "Walt's ideal for a town of tomorrow. . . . With Celebration, we're giving something back, trying to blaze a trail to improve American family life, education and health."[12] But there is more at stake in Disney's venture than simply acting out Walt's vision for urban renewal; there is also a postmodern appeal to a middle-class culture for which safety and security have become the chief values. In Disney culture, the community is not about self-rule but about adhering to the rules laid down by a central authority and legitimated through an appeal to the rewards of the marketplace, all of which have a Disney copyright. One such "reward" is decoupling the language of politics from the discourse of community and substituting security, conformity, and regulation—referred to in Disney language as "Family Friendly Planning"—for the risk-filled dynamics of democracy.[13] One example of the Disney vision of community is on display in a video offered to prospective Celebration home buyers. Set against the implied chaos of real urban space—read racial and class anarchy—it begins with a nostalgic and class-specific appeal: "There is a place that takes you back to that time of innocence. . . . A place of caramel apples and cotton candy, secret forts and hopscotch on the streets. That place is here again, in a new town called Celebration."[14]

Disney's nostalgia machine is premised on an appeal to a past that is safe and is predicated on the assumption that a viable public sphere is essentially middle class and white.

Community in this sense has little to do with the risk of building democratic structures, of creating cultural diversity, or of addressing pressing social problems and a great deal to do with the fantasy of social isolation—the luxury of not having to think about, or see, human suffering. Evan McKenzie argues that behind towns like Celebration is the notion that "I am going to leave America and go into this fantasy kingdom where there is no crime, with people only like me."[15] Frank Furedi suggests that there is more at stake here than a yearning to return to a more comfortable place; there is also the powerful workings of a corporate culture in which "personal safety is a growth industry. . . . Passions that were once devoted to a struggle to change the world (or keep it the same way) are now invested in trying to ensure that we are safe."[16]

The Walt Disney Company chose to open its $2.5 billion town on November 18, 1995, Mickey Mouse's birthday. Innocence, playfulness, and family life are the bait. But the motivation behind Celebration is far from innocent; it appears to be animated by Disney's rush toward a post-Fordist future of unregulated profit making. In the 1960s, Disney purchased 27,000 acres of land from the state of Florida at approximately $200 an acre. The company is now selling that land in quarter-acre lots for upward of $80,000. Developing this land has another positive spin-off: it makes Disney less attractive to corporate raiders, who would no longer be able to make a profit by developing the land.[17]

Banking on its reputation for doing things right, Disney invested heavily in the development of a quality school in Celebration. Investing in such a project was necessary for a number of reasons, including the fact that good schools attract home buyers, a fact recognized by reporters who have followed Disney's involvement with Celebration School. Leslie Postal, a newspaper reporter in Orlando, points out that Celebration School "is designed to be a showcase for high-tech and innovative instruction and is a drawing card for families building homes in the new town."[18] But Disney wasn't using the school merely to sell expensive homes; the company's investment in public education also provided another route through which it could continue to legitimate its interest in children while expanding its control over them as a potential market. Not only do kids provide a captive market open to the influence of a new electronic media technology—illustrated by the rise of Channel One—but Disney-sponsored schools provide the opportunity for producing cultural goods, texts, and entertainment and to claim that such commodities have educational value.

Although the K–12 schools are owned and operated by the Osceola County School District, the Walt Disney Company donated the land, the design services, and up to $22 million. Osceola has spent $18 million in taxpayers' money for the school and must come up with funding for its day-to-day operations. Stetson University also played a major role in the school by contributing to its curriculum development and offering leadership programs to teachers. A three-member board, representing the Osceola County School Board, the Disney Celebration Company, and Stetson University, manages the school. The Disney public relations machine describes the school as

> a unique public/private collaboration between the School District of Osceola County, Disney, and Stetson University. Students are taught in multi-age groups focusing on personalized learning plans and portfolios that incorporate authentic measures of success. The school facility supports interactive learning and provides innovative technology linkages for communication throughout the community and the world. Celebration School was developed in collab-

oration with many of the nation's leading educational visionaries and institutions, and serves as a model for other school districts across the nation.[19]

Other public relations information includes a list of fifteen education founding principles, such as "accountability," "celebration," "communication," "cooperation," "equity," "human dignity," and "wellness." Although they sound progressive, these principles read less as elements of a specifically defined educational vision than as a grab bag of attributes that would have general appeal to both conservative and liberal middle-class parents.

The public relations campaign also lists leading educators who were instrumental in developing the school's curriculum, methods, and leadership principles. Included in the group are Howard Gardner, a Harvard University professor of educational psychology who specializes in the subject of multiple intelligence; William Glasser, author of *Schools without Failure* and a strong advocate of schools as therapeutic agencies; and University of Minnesota professors David and Roger Johnson, who are advocates of cooperative learning. According to one Disney source, the challenge that the group was to address was framed by the question, What sort of school do we create to showcase the best ideas and practices in public education?

The answer that appeared in a *Disney* magazine article on Celebration School is suggestive: Gardner, Glasser, and the Johnsons "set to work researching the best practices in education—old and new. What emerged was a plan to help students find their most successful learning styles through, among other things, collaborative teaching, in which four to six teachers work together leading classes of 50 to 100 students, and collaborative learning, in which students work together, most often in teams of three or four."[20] The question challenging this group of educational theorists is provocative, but the answer appears to go no further than simply sanctioning a grab bag of methods. There was no attempt to understand teaching as a moral and political practice rather than simply a technical one nor to articulate a moral vision and a social ethics that would provide a referent for justifying particular pedagogical practices, teaching styles, and curriculum choices. Questions of meaning and purpose became technical questions unrelated to issues of power, politics, and possibility and unrelated to the way Celebration School might contribute to the social imagination of particular communities or expand the capacities that people need to exercise critical agency. The school's apparent emphasis on technical over civic competencies is, however, compatible with the pedagogical practices employed by the Disney corporation. Emphasizing the acquisition of skills over critical, ethical thinking, these educational sites produce students and workers trained to adapt to the world rather than to shape it. Moreover, the town of Celebration might be ill served by the production of a body of civic-minded youth, given the town's adherence to the principles of obedience, conformity, and passivity in the pursuit of the Disney utopia.

The notion of "best" is relative and contextual, and gains its meaning within the broader political and social considerations that it presupposes and reproduces. What is "best" for students becomes meaningful as a pedagogical project only when the following considerations are addressed: What kind of students does a school wish to produce? What is the ethical/political vision that defines meaningful knowledge, character, and practice? What vision of society and the future is presupposed in the teaching practices, social relations, values, and curricula legitimated by the school? In Disney's school there is no mention of public politics and its relationship to learning. Designed by Disney at the cost of nearly $20 million, the Celebration School is advertised as a showcase educational institution because of its distinctive organization, curriculum, and high technology. The school employs multiage, nongraded learning and organizes students into "neighborhoods," with approximately a hundred students and four teachers per neighborhood. The buildings housing the neighborhoods contain large open areas with computer workstations, teachers' offices, science labs, water fountains, and restrooms. Instead of traditional school furniture, there are cushioned window seats, brightly colored rugs, beanbag chairs, and a library with two beds on which kids can relax while reading. In the cafeteria windows are countertop computer hookups for laptop computers. The student-to-computer ratio is three to one; as the school secures more computers the ratio will get even smaller. The library contains a computerized central bank of videocassette recorders that allow students and teachers to have videos projected onto televisions, computers, or regular movie screens. There is even a space for desktop publishing. The emphasis is on creative and lifelong learning, and assessments and evaluations focus on student projects, portfolios, demonstrations, and exhibitions.

What is interesting about Disney's relationship with the school is that, on the surface, the school appears to be quite progressive and at odds with the elements of Disney culture and pedagogy that characterize Disney's other educational sites. Although there are hints of the traditional Disney emphasis on turning the practical task of learning into the stuff of adventure, the claim to progressivism is founded largely on the school's use of sophisticated technologies, interactive learning, personalized learning plans, and portfolio-based evaluation. But there is also the ideological underpinning, which is best understood through the experts Disney relied upon for the school's design, resources, and methods.

The experts whom Disney called upon to shape its curriculum are largely grounded in educational psychology and have little or nothing to say about the relationship between schools and society—about how power works through the various processes in which knowledge and authority are constructed to produce democratic identities—that is, engaged citizens prepared to expand and strengthen a critical democracy. Howard Gardner is particularly interesting on this. As an educational reformer, he has become known for his lifelong focus on multiple intelligence. An advocate of teachers' recognizing different styles of learning among students, he preaches the need for educators to teach forms of understanding through models provided by disciplinary-based subject matter experts. Gardner has parlayed his approach into a virtual industry; one can find advertisements for his videos, teaching guides, and books in everything from standard educational magazines to airline travel guides. Gardner's student-as-disciplinary-expert fits well with the emphasis on creating workers who are flexible, efficient, innovative, self-controlled, and collaborative. Understanding in this sense has less to do with critique than with problem solving, and the relationship between knowledge and power is addressed as a strategic issue rather than an ethical one. Knowledge means learning how to adapt to change; it emphasizes flexibility, speed, and innovation, not how to challenge substantive injustices in a society founded on deep inequalities.[21]

Another "expert" that the Disney school relied upon is William Glasser, who adds a psychotherapeutic dimension to Gardner's emphasis on multiple learning and understanding. For Glasser, the key to successful schooling is "creating an environment of warm, personal involvement among the teachers."[22] Human relations become the stuff of good schooling in this discourse, and there is a strong emphasis on the importance of a school culture that promotes self-discovery and relevance. The problem with this approach is that it often reproduces a "me-centered politics in which the search for meaning replaces the search for justice."[23] Relevance in this discourse becomes simply experiential and has little to do with politics and systemic relations of power. Abstracted from considerations of politics, pedagogies of relevance focus on deciphering students' needs so they can be redirected, monitored, and manipulated rather than focusing on what it means to educate students to become democratic subjects attentive to how the personal and the social interact as part of a larger network of power, governance, and critical agency.

Celebration School's staged philosophical emphasis on the cognitive and the therapeutic resonates with a broader public politics that aims to encourage critique, critical resistance, and public risk taking. Yet, at the same time, Disney's tradition of shutting down dissent in other cultural spheres under its control raises doubts about its willingness to support classroom practices and curricular policies that encourage students to challenge corporate power, critically interrogate media culture, engage in subversive readings of history, and dispute the role of people as mere spectators, consumers, and passive citizens. Would administrators and teachers at Celebration School ever show students *Mickey Mouse Goes to Haiti,* a twenty-eight-minute documentary "about the exploitation of workers in factories contracted to Disney"? Students at a Chicago school not only watched the film but protested Disney's practices in front of a local Disney Store—accompanied by their teachers![24] With its corporate empire to protect, the question is, To what degree will Disney provide an education that encourages students to develop the tools and citizenship skills to combat social problems?

Certainly, there are teachers in Celebration School who teach against the grain and who offer perspectives at odds with the Disney culture. But the issue is not to ensure that such resistance is possible but to recognize the limits of resistance in the face of overwhelming corporate power, whose history does not support a self-critical examination of its own abuses of power. This became evident when a group of Celebration School parents protested the school's progressive teaching methods. Rather than using such critiques to demonstrate how democracy works to foster exchange and dialogue, Disney claimed that the dissenters "had difficulty understanding the school's approach to teaching and grading."[25] In another instance, rather than taking seriously dissenters' concerns about curriculum structure and discipline, Disney officials claimed that many of the dissenting families were "just homesick for the towns they left."[26]

Brent Herrington, Celebration's community services manager, put out a newsletter soliciting contributions for the "positive parents fund," implying that those who did not support the progressive school curriculum were "negative parents."[27] The controversy over the school caused a number of families to decide to move out of Celebration. The only catch was that they had signed a contract stating that they could not sell their house for a profit if they had lived in it for less than a year. Disney agreed to suspend the rule "only on condition of signing an agreement promising never to reveal their reasons for leaving Celebration."[28] For one dissenting family, the Walt Disney Company "offered to help in selling the house and other incentives in return for a promise 'not to disclose to any third party' their reasons for leaving."[29] It seems that "the happiest place on earth" could view dissent only as a danger to the community and, in typical Disney fashion, attempted to use its corporate power to squelch that dissent. Not good news if public education is to be used to teach students about democracy.

There are other drawbacks to Disney's involvement with Celebration School. The Osceola County School District has invested close to $18 million in the school partnership with Disney, diverted from improving other schools in the district, which "suffer from leaking roofs, faulty wiring, and cramped quarters."[30] At present, 80 percent of the students who attend Celebration School are from the town, which means that the school will have little effect on the vast majority of minority kids enrolled in Florida's schools, many of which are underfunded. Mike Smith, the principal at Ventura Elementary School, views the Celebration School as a public relations venture that uses tax money to benefit a small number of middle-class kids: "We're starting a nice, little private school at Walt Disney World for people who have high incomes. Those kids are going to do well no matter where they are."[31]

CONCLUSION

We are witnessing in this country the decline of public culture and increased attacks on the most basic institutions of democratic public life. Public funding for the arts, backing for public schools, and support for social programs are in decline. Accompanying such a decline is a shift from public action to private concern, social welfare to individual initiative, and public good to self-interest. Corporate culture within the last decade has kindled the popular imagination with a discourse of reform that celebrates individualism, profits, and the culture of the market. Lost in this shift is the language of community, democracy, and the public good, a shift that undermines claims for public purpose, public service, and public education.

As the Walt Disney Company expands its corporate reach into everyday life, including its move into public schooling, it will not only undermine attempts to revitalize public education for all students, it will also sanitize and trivialize any serious engagement with public memory, citizenship, and democracy. Disney's educational and political influence in all aspects of society raises questions about turning over public culture—and civil society itself—to a totalizing corporate environment. The issue here is not whether people read Disney differently, or even enjoy the entertainment and commodities that the company dumps into the culture, but whether a democratic society will allow the corporate culture to blur the distinction between public and private, entertainment and history, critical citizenship and consumption. What are the implications for a democratic society increasingly under the sway of a corporate culture that subordinates political, public, and historical discourse and culture to the pleasures of consumption, escapist entertainment, and corporate profits?

NOTES

1. Mark Crispin Miller, "Free the Media," *Nation*, June 3, 1996, p. 9.

2. Raymond Williams, *Communications* (New York: Barnes and Noble, 1967), p. 15.

3. Donna Leinsing, "Building a Community of Excellence," *National Forum: Phi Kappa Phi Journal* 77:1 (1997), p. 31.

4. See "Disney's Programs Offer a Wide Range of Support," *Personnel Journal* (November 1992), p. 61.

5. Jennifer J. Laabs, "Disney Helps Keep Kids in School," *Personnel Journal* (November 1992), p. 66.

6. Michael Pollan, "Town-Building Is No Mickey Mouse Operation," *New York Times Magazine*, December 4, 1997, p. 58.

7. Tom Vanderbilt, "Mickey Mouse Goes to Town(s)," *Nation*, August 28/September 4, 1995, p. 197.

8. "Disney Tries to Create the Perfect Community . . . Blending Old and New in Celebration, Fla.," *CQ Researcher,* March 21, 1997, p. 254.

9. Mike Davis, *City of Quartz* (London: Verso, 1990), p. 224.

10. Pollan, "Town-Building," pp. 58–59.

11. Ibid., p. 78.

12. Ibid., p. 59.

13. Russ Rymer, "Back to the Future: Disney Reinvents the Company Town," *Harper's Magazine* (October 1996), p. 67.

14. Ibid., p. 68.

15. "Disney Tries to Create the Perfect Community," p. 255.

16. Frank Furedi, *Culture of Fear* (London: Cassell, 1997), p. 1.

17. Pollan, "Town-Building," p. 59.

18. Leslie Postal, "Celebration School Schedule Gets Boost: Disney and District Officials Work Out a Payment Plan to Avoid Postponing Construction," *Orlando Sentinel,* April 14, 1996, p. 1.

19. From a packet given to families moving to Celebration and to visitors.

20. Pippin Ross, "Celebrating Education," *Disney Magazine* (Fall 1997), p. 84.

21. For an excellent analysis of the relationship between cognitive science, especially the work of Howard Gardner and the demands of the new capitalism, see James Paul Gee, Glynda Hull, and Colin, Lankshear, *The New Work Order* (Boulder, Colo.: Westview, 1996), esp. chap. 3, "Alignments: Education and the New Capitalism."

22. William Glasser, *Schools without Failure* (New York: Harper and Row, 1969), p. 204.

23. Ronald Aronson, "The Meaning of Politics," *Dissent* (Spring 1998), p. 119.

24. Steven Friedman, "Taking Action against Disney," *Rethinking Schools* (Summer 1997), p. 18.

25. Ross, "Celebrating Education," p. 88.

26. Caroline E. Mayer, "At the Mickey House Club," *Washington Post, National Weekly Edition,* September 1, 1996, p. 17.

27. Pollan, "Town-Building," p. 76.

28. Ibid.

29. Steve Stecklow, "Disney's Model School: No Cause to Celebrate," *Wall Street Journal,* June 3, 1997, p. B10.

30. Leslie Postal, "Disney's Experiment in Education Takes Off," *Orlando Sentinel,* August 13, 1996, p. A1.

31. Ibid.

3

CHILDREN'S CULTURE AND DISNEY'S ANIMATED FILMS

Animation as a form of historical memory has entered real space. After all, any space or film that uses manipulated, interactive imagery must be called, by definition, a form of animation; and we are increasingly being submerged in life as a video game, even while our political crises deepen, and our class difference widens. . . . We act out stories inside cartoons now.

—Norman M. Klein, *Seven Minutes: The Life and Death of the American Animated Cartoon*

As a single father of three young boys, I found myself somewhat reluctantly being introduced to the world of Hollywood animated films and, in particular, to those produced by Disney. Before becoming an observer of this form of children's culture, I accepted the largely unquestioned assumption that animated films stimulate imagination and fantasy, create a feeling of innocence and healthy adventure, and in general are "good" for kids. In other words, such films appeared to be wholesome vehicles of amusement, a highly regarded source of fun and joy for children.

However, within a very short period of time, it became clear to me that these films do more than entertain.[1] Needless to say, animated films operate on many registers, but one of the most persuasive is the role they play as the new "teaching machines." I soon found that for my children, and I suspect for many others, these films possess at least as much cultural authority and legitimacy for teaching roles, values, and ideals as more traditional sites of learning, such as the public schools, religious institutions, and the family. Disney films combine enchantment and innocence in narrating stories that help children understand who they are, what societies are about, and what it means to construct a world of play and fantasy in an adult environment. The authority of such films, in part, stems from their unique form of representation and their ever-growing presence. But such authority is also produced and secured within a media apparatus equipped with dazzling technology, sound effects, and imagery packaged as entertainment, spin-off commercial products, and "huggable" stories.

The significance of Disney's animated films as a site of learning is heightened by the widespread recognition that schools and other public sites are increasingly beset by a crisis of vision, purpose, and motivation. The mass media, especially the world of Hollywood films, constructs a dreamlike world of security, coherence, and childhood innocence in which kids find a place to situate themselves in their emotional lives. Unlike the often hard, joyless reality of schooling, children's films provide a high-tech visual space in which adventure and pleasure meet in a fantasy world of possibilities and a commercial sphere of consumerism and commodification. The educational relevance of animated films became especially clear to me as my kids experienced the vast entertainment and teaching machine embodied by Disney. Increasingly, as I watched a number of Disney films first in the movie theater and then on video, I became aware of how necessary it was to move beyond treating these films as transparent entertainment and to question the diverse messages that constitute Disney's conservative view of the world.

TRADEMARKING INNOCENCE

Kids learn from Disney films, so maybe it's time parents and educators paid closer attention to what these films are saying. I realize that this heresy, especially at a time when kids are being subjected to increasing violence in Hollywood blockbusters, video games, and other commercial forms of entertainment. But while Disney films do not promote the violence that has become central to many other forms of popular and mass culture, they do carry cultural and social messages that need to be scrutinized. After all, "the happiest place on earth" has traditionally gained its popularity in part through its trademark image of innocence, which has largely protected it from the interrogation of critics.

Left-wing criticism of Disney is often ignored by the popular press. Yet the recent charge by conservative Southern Baptists that Disney films promote a seditious, anti-Christian ideology received enormous publicity in the mainstream media. The reason is that such criticism appears so extreme as to be comical and, therefore, safe for the media to cover. The more liberal critiques often ignore entirely the racist, sexist, and antidemocratic ethos that permeates Disney films. For instance, the *New York Times* critic Michiko Kakutani argues that if anything is wrong with Disney's animated films it is that the characters of late are too preachy and promote "wholesome messages" that "only an ogre or bigot could hate."[2] One can't help wondering what is wholesome about Disney's overt racism toward Arabs displayed in *Aladdin,* the retrograde gender roles at work in *The Little Mermaid* and *Beauty and the Beast,* and the undisguised celebration of antidemocratic governments and racism (remember the hyenas, who sounded like poor blacks and Hispanics?) evident in *The Lion King.* (I discuss these films in detail later in this chapter.)

There is more at work here than a successful public relations campaign intent on promoting Disney's claim to goodness and morality. There is also the reality of a powerful economic and political empire, which in 1997 made more than $22.5 billion in revenues from all of its divisions.[3] Disney is more than a corporate giant; it is also a cultural institution that fiercely protects its legendary status as purveyor of innocence and moral virtue.

Quick to mobilize its legal representatives, public relations spokespersons, and professional cultural critics to safeguard the borders of its "magic kingdom," Disney has aggressively prosecuted violations of its copyrights and has a reputation for bullying authors who use the Disney archives but refuse to allow Disney censors to approve their manuscripts before they are actually published.[4] For example, in its zeal to protect its image and extend its profits, Disney has threatened legal action against three South Florida day care centers for using Disney cartoon characters on their exterior walls. In this instance, Disney's role as an aggressive defender of conservative family values was undermined through its aggressive endorsement of property rights. While Disney's reputation as an undisputed moral authority on American values has taken a beating in the last few years, the power of Disney's mythological status cannot be underestimated.

Disney's image as an icon of American culture is consistently reinforced through the penetration of the Disney empire into every aspect of social life. Disney's $22 billion empire shapes children's experiences through box office movies, home videos, theme parks, hotels, sports teams, retail stores, classroom instructional films, compact discs, radio programs, television shows, internet servers, and family restaurants.[5] Through the use of public visual space, Disney's network of power relations promotes the construction of an all-encompassing world of enchantment allegedly free from ideology, politics, and power.[6] At the same time, Disney goes to great lengths to boost its civic image. Defining itself as a vehicle for education and civic responsibility, Disney has sponsored teacher of the year awards, provided Doer and Dreamer scholarships, and offered financial aid, internships, and other learning opportunities to disadvantaged urban youth through educational and work programs, such as its ice-skating program called Goals. Intent on defining itself as a purveyor of ideas rather than commodities, Disney is aggressively developing its image as a public service industry.[7] For example, Disney has become a partner in a public school venture in Celebration, Florida (see chap. 2). No longer content to spread its values through media entertainment and theme parks, Disney has now inserted itself into the growing lucrative market of the public school system.

What is interesting here is that Disney no longer simply dispenses the fantasies through which childhood innocence and adventure are produced, experienced, and affirmed. Disney now provides prototypes for families, schools, and communities. From the seedy urban haunts of New York City to the spatial monuments of consumption-shaping Florida, Disney is refiguring the social and cultural landscape while spreading its corporate ideology through the inventions of its imagineers. Disney transformed large sections of West Forty-second Street in New York City into an advertisement for a cleaned-up Disney version of America. It has also created the town of Celebration, Florida, designed after the "main streets of small-town America and reminiscent of Norman Rockwell images."[8] What Disney leaves out of its upbeat promotional literature is the rather tenuous notion of democracy that informs its view of municipal government, since Celebration is "premised upon citizens not having control over the people who plan for them and administer the policies of the city."[9]

But Disney does more than provide prototypes for up-scale communities; it also makes a claim on the future through its nostalgic view of the past. The French theorist Jean Baudrillard provides an interesting theoretical twist on the scope and power of Disney's influence, arguing that Disneyland is more "real" than fantasy because it now provides the image on which America constructs itself. For Baudrillard, Disneyland functions as a "deterrent" designed to "rejuvenate in reverse the fiction of the real." "Disneyland is there to conceal the fact that it is the 'real' country, all of 'real' America, which is Disneyland (just as prisons are there to conceal the fact that it is the social in its entirety, in its banal omnipresence, which is carceral). Disneyland is presented as imaginary in order to make us believe that the rest is real, when in fact all of Los Angeles and the America surrounding it are no longer real but of the order of the hyperreal and of simulation."[10] Examples of the Disnification of America abound. For instance, the Houston airport modeled its monorail after the one at Disneyland. New housing developments throughout America appropriate a piece of nostalgia by imitating the Victorian architecture of Disneyland's Main Street, USA. Moreover, throughout America, shopping malls imitate Disney's approach to retailing so "that shopping takes place in themed environments."[11] It seems that the real policy makers are not in Washington, D.C., but in California, and they call themselves the Disney imagineers. The boundaries between entertainment, education, and commercialization collapse through Disney's sheer reach into everyday life. The scope of the Disney empire reveals both shrewd business practices and a sharp eye for providing dreams and products through forms of popular culture in which kids are willing to materially and emotionally invest.

Popular audiences tend to reject any link between ideology and the prolific entertainment world of Disney. And yet Disney's pretense of innocence appears to some critics as little more than a promotional mask that covers its aggressive marketing techniques and its influence in educating children to become active consumers. Eric Smoodin, editor of *Disney Discourse,* a book critical of Disney's role in American culture, argues that "Disney constructs childhood so as to make it entirely compatible with consumerism."[12] Even more disturbing is the widespread belief that Disney's "innocence" renders it unaccountable for the way it shapes children's sense of reality: its sanitized notions of identity, difference, and history in the seemingly apolitical cultural universe of the "magic kingdom." Jon Wiener argues that Disneyland's version of Main Street America harks back to an "image of small towns characterized by cheerful commerce, with barbershop quartets and ice cream sundaes and glorious parades." For Wiener, this view not only fictionalizes and trivializes the real Main Streets of the turn of the century, it also appropriates the past to legitimate a portrayal of a world "without tenements or poverty or urban class conflict. . . . It's a native white Protestant dream of a world without blacks or immigrants."[13]

CRITIQUING DISNEY FILMS

Some of Disney's animated films produced since 1989 are important because they have received enormous praise from the dominant press and have achieved blockbuster status.[14] For many children, they represent an entrance into the world of Disney. Moreover, the financial success and popularity of these films, rivaling many adult films, do not engender the critical analyses that adult films usually do. In short, critics and audiences are more willing to suspend critical judgment about children's films. Animated fantasy and entertainment films appear to fall outside of the world of values, meaning, and knowledge often associated with documentaries, art films, and even wide-circulation adult films. Elizabeth Bell, Lynda Haas, and Laura Sells capture this sentiment: "Disney audiences . . . legal institutions, film theorists, cultural critics, and popular audiences all guard the borders of Disney film as 'off limits' to the critical enterprise, constructing Disney as a metonym for 'America'—clean, decent, industrious—'the happiest place on earth.' "[15]

Given the influence that the Disney ideology has on children, it is imperative for parents, teachers, and other adults to understand how such films influence the values of the children who view them. As a producer of children's culture, Disney should not be given an easy pardon because it is defined as a citadel of fun and good cheer. On the contrary, as one of the primary institutions constructing childhood culture in the United States, Disney warrants healthy suspicion and critical debate. Such a debate should not be limited to the home but should be centered in schools and other public sites of learning.

It is important not to address Disney's animated films by simply condemning Disney as an ideological reactionary corporation promoting a conservative worldview under the guise of entertainment. It is equally important not to celebrate Disney as the animated version of Mr. Rogers, doing nothing more than providing joy and happiness to children all over the world.[16] Disney does both. Disney does offer children visual stimulation and joy: dramatic thunderstorms, kaleidoscopic musical numbers, and the transformation of real life into wondrous spectacles. Disney's films offer children opportunities to locate themselves in a world that resonates with their desires and interests. Pleasure is one of the defining principles of what Disney produces, and children are both its subjects and objects. Hence, Disney's animated films have to be interrogated and mined as an important site for the production of children's culture. At the same time, these films are often filled with contradictory messages. Disney's influence and power must be situated within the broader understanding of the company's role as a corporate giant intent on spreading the conservative and commercial values that erode civil society while proclaiming to restructure it.

The role that Disney plays in shaping individual identities and in controlling the fields of social meaning through which children negotiate the world is far more complex than simple reactionary politics. If educators and other cultural workers are to include the culture of children as an important site of contestation and struggle, then it is imperative to analyze how Disney's animated films influence the way America's cultural landscape is imagined. Disney's scripted view of childhood and society needs to be engaged and challenged as "a historically specific matter of social analysis and intervention."[17] This is particularly important since Disney's animated films provoke and inform children's imaginations, desires, roles, and dreams while simultaneously sedimenting affect and meaning.

The wide distribution and popular appeal of Disney's animated films provide diverse audiences the opportunity for critical viewing. Critically analyzing how Disney films work to construct meaning, induce pleasure, and reproduce ideologically loaded fantasies is not meant as mere film criticism. Like any educational institution, Disney's view of the world needs to be discussed in terms of how it narrates children's culture and how it can be held accountable for what it does as a significant cultural public sphere—a space in which ideas, values, audiences, markets, and opinions create different publics and social formations. Of course, Disney's self-proclaimed innocence, inflexibility in dealing with social criticism, and paranoid attitude are now legendary and provide more reason that Disney be both challenged and engaged critically. Moreover, as a multibillion-dollar company, Disney's corporate and cultural influence is too enormous and far-reaching to allow it to define itself exclusively within the imaginary discourse of innocence, civic pride, and entertainment.[18]

The question of whether Disney's animated films are good for kids has no easy answer and resists simple analysis within the traditional and allegedly nonideological registers of fun and entertainment. Disney's most recent films—*The Little Mermaid* (1989), *Beauty and the Beast* (1991), *Aladdin* (1992), *The Lion King* (1994), *Pocahontas* (1995), *The Hunchback of Notre Dame* (1996), *Hercules* (1997), and *Mulan* (1998)—provide ample opportunity to address how Disney constructs a culture of joy and innocence for children out of the intersection of entertainment, advocacy, pleasure, and consumerism.[19] All of these films have been high-profile releases catering to massive audiences. Moreover, their commercial success is not limited to box-office profits. Successfully connecting consumption and moviegoing, Disney's animated films provide a "marketplace of culture," a launching pad for products and merchandise, including videocassettes, sound-track albums, children's clothing, furniture, stuffed toys, and new theme park rides.[20]

For example, *The Little Mermaid* and *Beauty and the Beast* videocassettes have combined sales of over 34 million. *Aladdin* has earned more than "$1 billion from box-office income, video sales and such ancillary baubles as Princess Jasmine dresses and Genie cookie jars"[21] and as a video interactive game sold more than 3 million copies in 1993. Similar sales are expected for the video and interactive game version of the film *The Lion King,* which had grossed $253.5 million in profits by August 24, 1994.[22] In fact, the first few weeks after *The Lion King* videocassette was released, it had sales of more than 20 million, and Disney's stock soared by $2.25 a share based on first-week revenues of $350 million. Jessica J. Reiff, an analyst at Oppenheimer and Company, says that "the movie will represent $1 billion in profits for Disney over two or three years."[23]

At the launching of *The Hunchback of Notre Dame,* Disney Records shipped 2 million sing-along home videos and seven *Hunchback* audio products, including the sound-track CD and cassette and a toddler-targeted *My First Read-Along.* Tie-in promotions for the film included Burger King, Payless Shoes, Nestle, and Mattel.[24] While *The Hunchback of Notre Dame* did not fare well at the box office, generating a disappointing $99 million in North American revenue, it is expected, according to *Adweek* magazine, "to generate $500 million in profit (not just revenues), after the other revenue streams are taken into account."[25] Similarly, Disney characters such as Mickey Mouse, Snow White, Jasmine, Aladdin, and Pocahontas have become prototypes for toys, logos, games, and rides that fill department stores all over the world. Disney theme parks, which made more than $4 billion in revenues in 1997, produced a sizable portion of their profits through the merchandising of toys based on characters from the animated films.

The Lion King has been one of Disney's biggest commercial successes and provided a model for marketing its future animated films, including *Mulan* and *Hercules* (with its blatant commercial built into the movie itself). *The Lion King* produced a staggering $1 billion in merchandizing profits in 1994 alone—the year of its release—not to mention the profits made from spin-off products. For example, when *The Lion King* was first released, Disney shipped out more than 3 million copies of the sound track.[26] Disney's culture of commercialism is big business and the toys modeled after Disney's animated films provide goods for the more than 728 Disney Stores worldwide. "The merchandise— Mermaid dolls, Aladdin undies, and collectibles like a sculpture of Bambi's Field Mouse—account for a stunning 20 percent of Disney's operating income."[27]

One of Disney's biggest promotion campaigns began with the summer 1995 release of *Pocahontas*. A record lineup of tie-in merchandise included Pocahontas stuffed animals, sheets, pillowcases, toothbrushes, games, moccasins, and more than forty "picture and activity books."[28] A consortium of corporations spent an estimated $125 million on cross-marketing *Pocahontas*. Two well-known examples include Burger King, which was converted into an advertisement for the film and gave away an estimated 50 million Pocahontas figurines, and the Mattel Corporation, which marketed more than fifty different dolls and toys.

But Disney's attempt to turn children into consumers and to make commodification a defining principle of children's culture should not suggest a parallel vulgarity in its aesthetic experiments with popular forms of representation. Disney has shown enormous inventiveness in its attempts to reconstruct the very grounds on which popular culture is defined and shaped. For example, by defining popular culture as a hybridized sphere that combines genres and forms and that often collapses the boundary between high and low culture, Disney has pushed against aesthetic form and cultural legitimacy. When *Fantasia* appeared in the 1930s, it drew the wrath of music critics, who, holding to an elite view of classical music, were outraged that the musical score drew from the canon of high culture. By combining high and low culture, Disney opened up new cultural possibilities for artists and audiences alike. Moreover, as sites of entertainment, Disney's films work because they put both children and adults in touch with joy and adventure. They present themselves as places to experience pleasure, even when we have to buy it. And yet Disney's brilliant use of aesthetic forms, musical scores, and inviting characters can only be read in light of the broader conceptions of reality shaped by these films within a wider system of dominant representations about gender roles, race, and agency that are endlessly repeated in the visual worlds of television, Hollywood film, and videocassettes.

A number of the films mentioned draw upon the talents of songwriters Howard Ashman and Alan Menken, whose skillful arrangements provide the emotional glue of the animation experience. The rousing calypso number "Under the Sea" in *The Little Mermaid,* and "Be Our Guest," the Busby Berkeley–inspired musical sequence in *Beauty and the Beast,* are indicative of the musical talent at work in Disney's animated film. Fantasy abounds, as Disney's animated films produce a host of exotic and stereotypical villains, heroes, and heroines. The Beast's enchanted castle in *Beauty and the Beast* becomes magical as household objects are transformed into dancing teacups and silverware and a talking teapot. And yet tied to the magical fantasy and lighthearted musical scores are stereotypes characteristic of Disney's view of childhood culture.

For example, Ursula, the large, oozing, black and purple squid in *The Little Mermaid*, gushes with evil and irony, and the heroine and mermaid, Ariel, appears as a cross between a typical rebellious teenager and a Southern California fashion model. Disney's representations of evil women and good women appear to have been fashioned in the editorial office of *Vogue*. The wolflike monster in *Beauty and the Beast* evokes a combination of terror and gentleness. Scar, in *The Lion King*, is a suave feline who masterfully portrays evil and betrayal. Disney's evocation of war and battle in *Mulan* is expansive and provocative. The animated objects and animals in these films are of the highest artistic standards, but they do not exist in an ideology-free zone. They are tied to larger narratives about freedom, rites of passage, intolerance, choice, greed, and the brutalities of male chauvinism.

Enchantment comes at a high price, however, if the audience is meant to suspend judgment of the films' ideological messages. Even though these messages can be read from a variety of viewpoints, the assumptions that structure these films restrict the number of cultural meanings that can be brought to bear on these films, especially when the intended audience is mostly children. The role of the critic of Disney's animated films, however, is not to assign them a particular ideological reading but to analyze the themes and assumptions that inform these films, both within and outside of the dominant institutional and ideological formations. Such analyses allow educators and others to understand how such films can become sites of contestation, translation, and exchange.

And beyond merely recognizing the plurality of readings such films might foster, there is also the pedagogical task of provoking audiences to reflect upon the ways in which Disney's themes function as part of a broader public discourse, privileging some definitions or interpretations over others. The conservative values that Disney films promote assume such force because of the context in which they are situated and because they resonate so powerfully with dominant perceptions and meanings. Pedagogically, this suggests the need for educators, parents, and others to analyze critically how the privileged dominant readings of Disney's animated films generate and affirm particular pleasures, desires, and subject positions that define for children specific notions of agency and its possibilities in society.

Contexts mold interpretations; but political, economic, and ideological contexts also produce the texts to be read. The focus on films must be supplemented with an analysis of the institutional practices and social structures that work to shape such texts| Such analysis should suggest pedagogical strategies for understanding how dominant regimes of power limit the range of views that children might bring to reading Disney's animated films. By making the relationship between power and knowledge visible, while simultaneously referencing what is often taken for granted, teachers and critics can analyze Disney's animated films pedagogically so that students and others can read such films within, against, and outside of the dominant codes that inform them.

There is a double pedagogical movement here. First, there is the need to read Disney's films in relation to their articulation with other dominant texts in order to assess their similarities in legitimating particular ideologies. Second, there is the need to use Disney's thematization of America and America's thematization of Disney as referents to make visible—and to disrupt—dominant codings and to do so in a space that invites dialogue, debate, and alternative readings. For instance, one major pedagogical challenge is to assess how dominant ideas that are repeated over time in these films and that are reinforced through other popular cultural texts can be taken as referents for engaging children in defining themselves within such representations. The task here is to provide readings of such films to serve as pedagogical referents.[29] By providing a theoretical referent for engaging Disney films, it becomes possible to explore pedagogically how we both construct and defend the readings we actually bring to such films, providing an opportunity to expand the dialogue regarding what Disney's films mean while simultaneously challenging the assumptions underlying dominant readings of these films. Taking a position on Disney's films should not degenerate into a doctrinaire reading or legitimate a form of political or pedagogical indoctrination with children or anybody else. Rather, such an approach should address how any reading of these films is ideological and should be engaged in terms of the context, the content, and the values and social relations it endorses. Moreover, engaging such readings politically and ideologically provides the pedagogical basis for making the films problematic and, thus, open to dialogue, rather than treating them uncritically, as mere entertainment.

WHAT CHILDREN LEARN FROM DISNEY

The construction of gender identity for girls and women represents one of the most controversial issues in Disney's animated films.[30] In both *The Little Mermaid* and *The Lion King,* the female characters are constructed within narrowly defined gender roles. All of the female characters in these films are ultimately subordinate to males and define their power and desire almost exclusively in terms of dominant male narratives. For instance, modeled after a slightly anorexic Barbie doll, Ariel, the mermaid in *The Little Mermaid*, at first glance appears to be engaged in a struggle against parental control, motivated by the desire to explore the human world and willing to take a risk in defining the subject and object of her desires. But, in the end, the struggle to gain independence from her father, Triton, and the desperate striving that motivates her dissolve when Ariel makes a Mephistophelian pact with the sea witch, Ursula. In this trade, Ariel gives away her voice to gain a pair of legs so that she can pursue the handsome prince, Eric.

Although girls might be delighted by Ariel's teenage rebelliousness, they are strongly positioned to believe, in the end, that desire, choice, and empowerment are closely linked to catching and loving a handsome man. Bonnie Leadbeater and Gloria Lodato Wilson explore the pedagogical message at work in the film: "The 20th-century innocent and appealing video presents a high-spirited role for adolescent girls, but an ultimately subservient role for adult women. Disney's 'Little Mermaid' has been granted her wish to be part of the new world of men, but she is still flipping her fins and is not going too far. She stands to explore the world of men. She exhibits her new-found sexual desires. But the sexual ordering of women's roles is unchanged."[31] Ariel becomes a metaphor for the traditional housewife in the making. When Ursula tells Ariel that taking away her voice is not so bad because men don't like women who talk, the message is dramatized when the prince attempts to bestow the kiss of true love on Ariel even though she has never spoken to him. Within this rigid narrative, womanhood offers Ariel the reward of marrying the right man for renouncing her former life under the sea. It is a cultural model for the universe of female choices in Disney's worldview.

The rigid gender roles in *The Little Mermaid* are not isolated instances in Disney's filmic universe; on the contrary, Disney's negative stereotypes about women and girls gain force through the way in which similar messages are consistently circulated and reproduced, to varying degrees, in many of Disney's animated films. For example, in *Aladdin* the issue of agency and power is centered primarily on the role of the young street tramp, Aladdin. Jasmine, the princess he falls in love with, is simply an object of his immediate desire as well as a social stepping-stone. Jasmine's life is almost completely defined by men, and, in the end, her happiness is ensured by Aladdin, who is finally given permission to marry her.

Disney's gender theme becomes a bit more complicated in *Beauty and the Beast, Pocahontas,* and *Mulan.* Belle, the heroine of *Beauty and the Beast,* is portrayed as an independent woman stuck in a provincial village in eighteenth-century France. Seen as odd because she always has her nose in a book, she is pursued by Gaston, the ultimate vain, macho male typical of Hollywood films of the 1980s. To Belle's credit, she rejects him, but in the end she gives her love to the Beast, who holds her captive in the hope that she will fall in love with him and break the evil spell cast upon him as a young man. Belle not only falls in love with the Beast, she "civilizes" him by instructing him on how to eat properly, control his temper, and dance. Belle becomes a model of etiquette and style as she turns this narcissistic, muscle-bound tyrant into a "new" man, one who is sensitive, caring, and loving. Some critics have labeled Belle a Disney feminist because she rejects and vilifies Gaston, the ultimate macho man.

Less obviously, *Beauty and the Beast* also can be read as a rejection of hypermasculinity and a struggle between the sensibilities of Gaston and the reformed sexist, the Beast. In this reading, Belle is less the focus of the film than a prop or "mechanism for solving the Beast's dilemma."[32] Whatever subversive qualities Belle personifies in the film, they seem to dissolve when focused on humbling male vanity. In the end, Belle simply becomes another woman whose life is valued for solving a man's problems.

Disney's next femme fatale, Pocahontas, appears to both challenge and reproduce some of these stereotypes. Rather than a young adolescent, Pocahontas is made over historically to resemble a shapely, contemporary, high-fashion supermodel. Bright, courageous, literate, and politically progressive, she is a far cry from the traditional negative stereotypes of Native Americans portrayed in Hollywood films. But Pocahontas's character, like that of many of Disney's female protagonists, is drawn primarily in relation to the men who surround her. Initially, her identity is defined in resistance to her father's attempts to marry her off to one of the bravest warriors in the tribe. But her coming-of-age identity crisis is largely defined by her love affair with John Smith, a blond colonist who looks like he belongs in a Southern California pinup magazine of male surfers. Pocahontas's character is drawn primarily through her struggle to save John Smith from being executed by her father. Pocahontas exudes a kind of soppy romanticism that not only saves John Smith's life but also convinces the crew of the British ship to rebel against its greedy captain and return to England.

Of course, this is a Hollywood rewrite of history that bleaches colonialism of its genocidal legacy. No mention is made of the fact that John Smith's countrymen would ultimately ruin Pocahontas's land, bring disease, death, and poverty to her people, and eventually destroy their religion, economic livelihood, and way of life. In the Disney version of history, colonialism never happened, and the meeting between the old and new worlds is simply fodder for another "love conquers all" narrative. One wonders how this film would have been viewed by the public if it had been about a Jewish woman who falls in love with a blond Aryan Nazi while ignoring any references to the Holocaust.

The issue of female subordination returns with a vengeance in *The Lion King*. All of the rulers of the kingdom are men, reinforcing the assumption that independence and leadership are tied to patriarchal entitlement and high social standing. The dependency that the beloved lion king, Mufasa, engenders in the women of Pride Rock is unaltered after his death, when the evil Scar assumes control of the kingdom. Lacking any sense of outrage, independence, or resistance, the women felines hang around to do Scar's bidding.

The gender stereotyping is somewhat modified in *Mulan*. The lead character of the same name is presented as a bold female warrior who challenges traditional stereotypes of young women. But for all of her independence, in the end, the film is, as the film critic Janet Maslin points out, "still enough of a fairy tale to need a Mr. Right."[33] Mulan may be an independent, strong-willed young woman, but the ultimate payoff for her bravery comes in the form of catching the handsome son of a general. And if the point is missed, when the heroine's grandmother first sees the young man as he enters Mulan's house, she affirms what she (the audience?) sees as Mulan's real victory, which is catching a man, and yells out: "Sign me up for the next war!" And there is another disturbing side to Mulan as an alleged strong woman. Rather than aligning herself against the patriarchal celebration of war, violence, and militarism, Mulan becomes a cross-dresser who proves that when it comes to war she can perform as well as any male. By embracing a masculine view of war, Mulan cancels out any rupturing of traditional gender roles. She simply becomes one of the boys. But lest the fantasy be taken too far, Disney reminds us at the conclusion of the film that Mulan is still just a girl in search of a man, and as in so many other Disney animated films, Mulan becomes an exoticized version of the All-American girl who manages to catch the most handsome boy on the block, square jaw and all.

Given Disney's purported obsession with family values, especially as a consuming unit, it is curious that, with the exception of *Mulan,* there are no strong mothers or fathers in these films.[34] Not only are powerful mothers absent, but with the exception of the fathers of Pocahontas and Mulan, all of the father figures are portrayed as weak or stupid. Only the mermaid has a domineering father. Jasmine's father is outwitted by his aides, and Belle's father is an airhead.

Jack Zipes, a leading theorist on fairy tales, claims that Disney's animated films reproduce "a type of gender stereotyping . . . that has an adverse effect on children, in contrast to what parents think. . . . Parents think they're essentially harmless—and they're not harmless."[35]

Racial stereotyping is another major issue in Disney films. There is a long history of racism associated with Disney, tracing back to *Song of the South,* released in 1946, and *The Jungle Book,* which appeared in 1967.[36] Moreover, racist representations of Native Americans as violent "redskins" were featured in Frontierland in the 1950s.[37] In addition, the main restaurant in Frontierland featured an actor representing the former slave Aunt Jemima, who would sign autographs for the tourists outside of her "Pancake House." Eventually, the exhibits and the Native Americans running them were eliminated by Disney executives because the

"Indian" canoe guides wanted to unionize. They were displaced by robotic dancing bears. Complaints from civil rights groups got rid of the degrading Aunt Jemima spectacle.[38]

One of the most controversial examples of racist stereotyping facing the Disney publicity machine occurred with the release of *Aladdin* in 1992, although such stereotyping reappeared in full force in 1994 with the release of *The Lion King. Aladdin* is a particularly important example because it was a high-profile release, the winner of two Academy Awards, and one of the most successful Disney films ever produced. The film's opening song, "Arabian Nights," begins its depiction of Arab culture with a decidedly racist tone. The lyrics of the offending stanza state: "Oh I come from a land/From a faraway place/Where the caravan camels roam./Where they cut off your ear/If they don't like your face./It's barbaric, but hey, it's home." A politics of identity and place associated with Arab culture magnified popular stereotypes already primed by the media through its portrayal of the Gulf War. Such a racist representation is furthered by a host of grotesque, violent, and cruel supporting characters.

Yousef Salem, a former spokesperson for the South Bay Islamic Association, characterized the film in the following way: "All of the bad guys have beards and large, bulbous noses, sinister eyes and heavy accents, and they're wielding swords constantly. Aladdin doesn't have a big nose; he has a small nose. He doesn't have a beard or a turban. He doesn't have an accent. What makes him nice is they've given him this American character. . . . I have a daughter who says she's ashamed to call herself an Arab, and it's because of things like this."[39] Jack Shaheen, a professor of broadcast journalism at Southern Illinois University, Edwardsville, along with the radio personality Casey Kasem, mobilized a public relations campaign protesting the anti-Arab themes in *Aladdin*. At first, Disney executives ignored the protest, but responding to the rising tide of public outrage agreed to change one line of the stanza in the subsequent videocassette and worldwide film release. Disney did not change the lyrics on its popular CD release of *Aladdin*.[40]

Disney executives were not unaware of the racist implications of the lyrics when they were first proposed. Howard Ashman, who wrote the title song, submitted an alternative set of lyrics when he delivered the original lines. The alternative lyrics, "Where it's flat and immense/And the heat is intense" eventually replaced the original verse, "Where they cut off your ear/If they don't like your face." Though the new lyrics appeared in the videocassette release of *Aladdin,* the line "It's barbaric, but hey, it's home" was not altered. More important, the mispronunciation of Arab names in the film, the racial coding of accents, and the use of nonsensical scrawl as a substitute for an actual written Arabic language were not removed.[41]

Racism in Disney's animated films is also evident in racially coded language and accents. For example, *Aladdin* portrays the "bad" Arabs with thick, foreign accents, while the Anglicized Jasmine and Aladdin speak in standard American English. A hint of the racism that informs this depiction is provided by Peter Schneider, president of feature animation at Disney at the time, who points out that Aladdin was modeled after Tom Cruise.

Racially coded representations and language are also evident in *The Lion King*. Scar, the icon of evil, is darker than the good lions. Moreover, racially coded language is evident, as the members of the royal family speak with posh British accents while Shenzi and Banzai, the despicable hyena storm troopers, speak with the voices of Whoopi Goldberg and Cheech Marin in the jive accents of a decidedly urban black or Hispanic youth. Disney falls back upon the same racial formula in *Mulan*. Not far removed from the Amos 'n' Andy crows in *Dumbo* is the racialized low-comedy figure of Mushu, a tiny red dragon with a black voice (Eddie Murphy). Mushu is a servile and boastful clown who seems unsuited to a mythic fable about China. He is the stereotype of the craven, backward, Southern, chitlin-circuit character that appears to feed the popular racist imagination. Racially coded language can also be found in an early version of *The Three Little Pigs*, in *Song of the South*, and in *The Jungle Book*.[42] These films produce representations and codes through which children are taught that characters who do not bear the imprint of white, middle-class ethnicity are culturally deviant, inferior, unintelligent, and a threat.

The racism in these films is defined by both the presence of racist representations and the absence of complex representations of African Americans and other people of color. At the same time, whiteness is universalized through the privileged representation of middle-class social relations, values, and linguistic practices. Moreover, the representational rendering of history, progress, and Western culture bears a colonial legacy that seems perfectly captured by Edward Said's notion of orientalism—a particular form of Western imperialism that shapes dominant thinking about the Orient—and its dependency on new images of centrality and sanctioned narratives.[43] Cultural differences are expressed through a "natural" racial hierarchy, which is antithetical to a viable democratic society. There is nothing innocent in what kids learn about race as portrayed in the "magical world" of Disney. Even in a film such as *Pocahontas*, in which cultural differences are portrayed more positively, there is the suggestion in the end that racial identities must remain separate. *Pocahontas* is one of the few love stories in Disney's animated series in which the lovers do not live together happily ever after. It is also one of the few love stories that brings lovers from different races together.

Another feature common to many of Disney's recent animated films is the celebration of antidemocratic social relations. Nature and the animal kingdom provide the mechanism for presenting and legitimating caste, royalty, and structural inequality as part of the natural order. The seemingly benign presentation of celluloid dramas, in which men rule, strict discipline is imposed through social hierarchies, and leadership is a function of one's social status, suggests a yearning for a return to a more rigidly stratified society, one modeled after the British monarchy of the eighteenth and nineteenth centuries. In Disney's animated films, "harmony is bought at the price of domination. . . . No power or authority is implied except for the natural ordering mechanisms" of nature.[44] For children, the messages suggest that social problems such as the history of racism, the genocide of Native Americans, the prevalence of sexism, and the crisis of democracy are simply willed through the laws of nature.

CONCLUSION

Given the corporate reach, cultural influence, and political power that Disney exercises over multiple levels of children's culture, Disney's animated films should be neither ignored nor censored by those who dismiss the conservative ideologies they produce and circulate. There are a number of issues to be addressed regarding the forging of a pedagogy and a politics responsive to Disney's shaping of children's culture. Below, I suggest how cultural workers, educators, and parents might critically engage Disney's influence in shaping the "symbolic environment into which our children are born and in which we all live out our lives."[45]

First, it is crucial that the realm of popular culture that Disney increasingly invades to teach values and to sell goods to children be taken seriously as a site of learning and contestation. This means, at the very least, that those cultural texts that dominate children's culture, including Disney's animated films, should be incorporated into school curricula as objects of social knowledge and critical analysis. This would entail a reconsideration of what counts as useful knowledge and offer theoretical suggestions for addressing the ways in which popular media aimed at shaping children's culture are implicated in power/knowledge relationships. This is not simply a call for making media literacy a part of what kids gain from school (as crucial as such a pedagogy is)[46] but a reconsideration of what counts as school knowledge. In simple terms, this means making popular culture an essential object of social analysis in schools.

Second, parents, community groups, educators, and other concerned individuals must be attentive to the diverse messages in Disney films in order both to criticize them when necessary and, more important, to reclaim them for more productive ends. At the very least, we must be attentive to the processes whereby meanings are produced in these films and how they work to secure particular forms of authority and social relations. At stake pedagogically is the issue of paying "close attention to the ways in which [such films] invite (or indeed seek to prevent) particular meanings and pleasures."[47] In fact, Disney's films appear to assign, quite unapologetically, rigid roles to women and people of color. Similarly, such films generally produce a narrow view of family values coupled with a nostalgic and conservative view of history that should be challenged and transformed. Educators need to take seriously Disney's attempt to shape collective memory, particularly when such attempts are unabashedly defined by one of Disney's imagineers in the following terms: "What we create is a sort of 'Disney realism,' sort of Utopian in nature, where we carefully program out all the negative, unwanted elements and program in the positive elements."[48] Disney's rendering of entertainment and spectacle, whether expressed in Frontierland, Main Street, USA, or its video and film productions, is not merely an edited, sanitary, and nostalgic view of history, one that is free of poverty, class differences, and urban decay. Disney's writing of public memory also aggressively constructs a monolithic notion of national identity that treats subordinate groups as either exotic or irrelevant to American history, simultaneously marketing cultural differences within "histories that corporations can live with."[49] Disney's version of U.S. history is not innocent, nor can it be dismissed as simply entertainment.

Disney's celluloid view of children's culture often works to strip the past, present, and future of diverse narratives and multiple possibilities, a rendering that needs to be revealed as a historically specific and politically constructed cultural "landscape of power." Rustom Bharacuha argues that "the consumption of . . . images . . . can be subverted through a particular use in which we are compelled to think through images rather than respond to them with a hallucinatory delight."[50] The images that pervade Disney's production of children's culture, along with their claim to public memory, need to be challenged and rewritten, "moved about in different ways," and read differently as part of the script of democratic empowerment.[51] It is within the drama of animated storytelling that children are often positioned pedagogically to learn what subject positions are open to them and what positions are not. Hence, the struggle over children's culture should be considered as part of a struggle over the related discourses of citizenship, national identity, and democracy itself.

Third, if Disney's films are to be viewed as more than narratives of fantasy and escape, becoming sites of reclamation and imagination that affirm rather than deny the long-standing relationship between entertainment and pedagogy, it is important to consider how we might insert the political and pedagogical back into the discourse of entertainment. In part, this points to analyzing how entertainment can be addressed as a subject of intellectual engagement rather than as a series of sights and sounds that wash over us. This suggests a pedagogical approach to popular culture that asks how a politics of the popular works to mobilize desire, stimulate imagination, and produce forms of identification that can become objects of dialogue and critical investigation. At one level, this suggests addressing the utopian possibilities in which children often find representations of their hopes and dreams. But it also suggests recognizing the pedagogical importance of what kids bring with them to the classroom (or to any other site of learning) as crucial both to decentering power in the classroom and to expanding the possibility of teaching students multiple literacies, as part of a broader strategy of teaching them to read the world critically.

We must pay attention to how these Disney films and visual media are used and understood differently by different kids. We must talk to children about these films so we can better understand how kids identify with them and what issues they raise, developing a language of pleasure and criticism. This suggests that we develop new ways of critically understanding and reading electronically produced visual media. Teaching and learning the culture of the book is no longer the staple of what it means to be literate. Children learn from exposure to popular cultural forms, which provide a new cultural register of what it means to be literate. This suggests a cultural pedagogy, rooted in cultural practices, that utilizes students' knowledge and experience of popular cultural forms. Students should be taught to critically analyze the messages produced by the electronically mediated popular culture, but they must also be able to master the skills and technology to produce these forms, making their own films, videos, and music. Thus a cultural pedagogy also requires more resources for schools and other sites of learning, providing the conditions for students and others to become the subject, not simply the object, of pedagogical work. Asserting their role as cultural producers is crucial if students are to become attentive to the workings of power, solidarity, and difference.

Fourth, Disney's reach into the spheres of economics, consumption, and culture suggest that we analyze Disney within a broad and complex range of relations of power. Eric Smoodin argues that the American public needs to "gain a new sense of Disney's importance, because of the manner in which his work in film and television is connected to other projects in urban planning, ecological politics, product merchandising, United States domestic and global policy formation, technological innovation, and constructions of national character."[52] This suggests undertaking analyses of Disney that connect, rather than separate, the various social and cultural formations in which the company engages. Clearly, such a dialectical practice not only provides a more theoretically accurate understanding of the reach and influence of Disney's power but also contributes to forms of analysis that discount the no-

tion that Disney is primarily about the pedagogy of entertainment.

Questions of ownership, control, and public participation in deciding how cultural resources are used should become a central issue in addressing the world of Disney and
other corporate conglomerates that shape cultural policy.
The control, production, and distribution of such films
should be analyzed as part of a wider circuit of power. In
this context, Disney's influence in the shaping of children's
culture cannot be reduced to critically interpreting the
ideas and values Disney promotes. Any viable analysis of
Disney must also confront the institutional and political
power Disney exercises through its massive control over diverse sectors of what Mark Crispin Miller calls the "national entertainment state."53 The availability, influence,
and cultural power of Disney's children's films demand
that they become part of a broader political discourse regarding who makes cultural policy. Issues regarding how
and what children learn could be addressed through public
debates about how the distribution and control of cultural
and economic resources ensure that children are exposed
to alternative narratives about themselves and the larger
society.

When the issue of children's culture is taken up by—and
shaped in—the public schools, it is assumed that this is a
matter of public policy and intervention. But when children's culture is shaped in the commercial sphere, the discourse of public intervention gets lost in abstract appeals to
the imperatives of the market and free speech. Free speech
is only as good as the democratic framework that makes
possible the extension of its benefits to all individuals,
groups, and public spheres. Treating Disney as part of a
media sphere that needs to be democratized and held accountable for the ways in which it wields power and manu-
factures social identities needs to be part of the discourse of

pedagogical analysis and public policy intervention. This type of analysis and intervention is perfectly suited for cultural theorists and community activists willing to employ an interdisciplinary approach to such an undertaking, to address popular culture as an object of serious analysis, to make the pedagogical a defining principle of such work, and to insert the political into the center of such projects.[54]

This suggests that cultural workers need to readdress a politics of representation and the discourse of political economy, treating their varied interrelations as a form of cultural work that rejects the material/cultural divide. The result would be an understanding of how such modalities inform each other within different contexts and across national boundaries. It is particularly important for cultural workers to understand how Disney films work as teaching machines within and across public cultures and social formations. Within this type of analysis, the messages, emotional investments, and ideologies produced by Disney can be traced through the circuits of power that both legitimate and insert "the culture of the Magic Kingdom" into multiple and overlapping public spheres. Disney films need to be analyzed not only for what they say but also for how they are apprehended by audiences within their national and international contexts. That is, cultural workers need to study these films intertextually and from a transnational perspective. Disney is not ignorant of different contexts; on the contrary, its power, in part, rests with its ability to address different contexts and to be read differently in different transnational formations. Disney engenders what Inderpal Grewa and Caren Kaplan call "scattered hegemonies."[55] It is precisely by addressing how these hegemonies operate in particular spaces of power, specific localities—in different transnational locations—that we will be able to understand the agendas and the politics at work.

The defeat in 1995 of Disney's proposed 3,000-acre theme park in Virginia suggests that Disney can be challenged and held accountable for the so-called Disnification of American culture. In this instance, a coalition of historians, community activists, educators, and other concerned groups mobilized against the land developers supporting the project, wrote articles against Disney's trivializing of history and its implications for the park, and aroused public opinion enough to generate an enormous amount of adverse criticism against the Disney project. What was initially viewed as merely a project for bringing a Disney version of fun and entertainment to hallowed Civil War grounds in historic Virginia was translated by opposition groups into a cultural struggle. And Disney lost.

What the Virginia cultural civil war suggests is that, although it is indisputable that Disney provides both children and adults with entertainment and pleasure, Disney's public responsibility does not end there. Rather than being viewed as a commercial venture innocently distributing pleasure to young people, the Disney empire must be seen as a pedagogical and policy-making enterprise actively engaged in the cultural landscaping of national identity and the "schooling" of the minds of young children. This is not to suggest that there is something sinister behind what Disney does. It points only to the need to address the role of fantasy, desire, and innocence in securing particular ideological interests, legitimating specific social relations, and making a claim on the meaning of public memory. Disney needs to be held accountable, which will require that parents, educators, and others challenge and disrupt both the institutional power and the images, representations, and values offered by Disney's teaching machine.

NOTES

1. For a critical engagement of commercialization, popular culture, and children's culture, see Marsha Kinder, *Playing with Power in Movies, Television, and Video Games* (Berkeley: University of California Press, 1991); Doug Kellner, *Media Culture* (New York: Routledge, 1995); David Buckingham and Julian Sefton-Green, *Cultural Studies Goes to School* (Washington, D.C.: Taylor and Francis, 1994).

2. Michiko Kakutani, "This Mouse Once Roared," *New York Times Magazine,* January 4, 1998, p. 8. Compare Kakutani's analysis with Matt Roth, "A Short History of Disney-Fascism," *Jump Cut,* no. 40 (1996), pp. 15–20.

3. Michael D. Eisner, "Letter to Shareholders," *The Walt Disney Company 1997 Annual Report* (Burbank, Calif.: Walt Disney Company, 1997), p. 2.

4. There is a growing list of authors who have been pressured by Disney either through its refusal to allow copyrighted materials to be used or through its influence on publishers. Examples can be found in Jon Wiener, "In the Belly of the Mouse: The Dyspeptic Disney Archives," *Lingua Franca* (July/August 1994), pp. 69–72. Also Jon Wiener, "Murdered Ink," *Nation,* May 31, 1993, pp. 743–50. One typical example occurred with a book in which one of my own essays on Disney appears. While editing a book critical of Disney, Elizabeth Bell, Lynda Haas, and Laura Sells requested permission from Disney executives to use the Disney archives. In response, the editors received a letter from one of Disney's legal assistants asking to approve the book. The editors declined, and Disney forbade the use of its name in the title of the book and threatened to sue if the Disney name was used. Indiana University Press argued that it did not have the resources to fight Disney, so the title of the book was changed from *Doing Disney* to *From Mouse to Mermaid.* In another instance, Routledge publishers omitted an essay by David Kunzle on the imperialist messages in Disney's foreign comics in a book entitled *Disney Dis-*

course. Thinking that Disney would not provide permission for the use of illustrations from the Disney archives, Routledge decided they could not publish the essay. Discouraged, Kunzle said, "I've given up. I'm not doing any more work on Disney. I don't think any university press would take the risk. The problem is not the likelihood of Disney winning in court, it's the threat of having to bear the cost of fighting them." Wiener, "In the Belly of the Mouse," p. 72.

5. This figure comes from Michael Meyer et al., "Of Mice and Men," *Newsweek,* September 5, 1994, p. 41.

6. The mutually determining relationship of culture and economic power is captured in Sharon Zukin, *Landscapes of Power: From Detroit to Disney World* (Berkeley: University of California Press, 1991), p. 221:

> The domestication of fantasy in visual consumption is inseparable from centralized structures of economic power. Just as the earlier power of the state illuminated public space—the streets—by artificial lamplight, so the economic power of CBS, Sony, and the Disney Company illuminates private space at home by electronic images. With the means of production so concentrated and the means of consumption so diffused, communication of these images becomes a way of controlling both knowledge and imagination, a form of corporate social control over technology and symbolic expressions of power.

7. For a listing of public service programs that Disney has initiated, see Jennifer J. Laabs, "Disney Helps Keep Kids in School," *Personnel Journal* (November 1992), pp. 58–68.

8. Disney executives, quoted in Mark Walsh, "Disney Holds Up School as Model for Next Century," *Education Week* 39, (1994), p. 1.

9. Tom Vanderbilt, "Mickey Mouse Goes to Town(s)," *Nation,* August 28/September 4, 1995, p. 199.

10. Jean Baudrillard, *Simulations* (New York: Semiotext(e), 1983), p. 25. Also see Baudrillard, "Consumer Society," in Mark

Poster, ed., *Jean Baudrillard: Selected Works* (Stanford: Stanford University Press, 1988), pp. 29–56.

11. Alan Bryman, *Disney and His Worlds* (New York: Routledge, 1995), p. 26.

12. Eric Smoodin, "How to Read Walt Disney," in Smoodin, ed., *Disney Discourse: Producing the Magic Kingdom* (New York: Routledge, 1994), p. 18.

13. Jon Wiener, "Tall Tales and True," *Nation,* January 31, 1994, p. 134.

14. Disney's animated film *The Lion King* may be the most financially successful film ever made. Disney's animated films released since 1990 are all among the ten top-grossing films. *The Lion King* ranked first, with $253.5 million; *Aladdin* ranked second, with $217.4 million; and *Beauty and the Beast* ranked seventh, grossing $145.9 million. See Thomas King, "Creative but Unpolished Top Executive for Hire," *Wall Street Journal,* August 26, 1994, p. B1.

15. Elizabeth Bell, Lynda Haas, and Laura Sells, "Walt's in the Movies," in Bell, Haas, and Sells, eds., *From Mouse to Mermaid* (Bloomington: Indiana University Press, 1995), p. 3.

16. The celebrations of Walt Disney are too numerous to mention in detail, but an early example is Bob Thomas, *Walt Disney: An American Original* (New York: Simon and Schuster, 1976). Thomas's book followed on the heels of a scathing attack on Disney by Richard Schickel, *The Disney Version* (New York: Simon and Schuster, 1968). A more recent version of the no-holds-barred critique of Disney is Carl Hiassen, *Team Rodent: How Disney Devours the World* (New York: Ballantine, 1998). The more moderate position is Steven Watts, *The Magic Kingdom* (New York: Houghton Mifflin, 1998). Schickel's book is one of the best critiques of Disney.

17. Barbara Foley, "Subversion and Oppositionality in the Academy," in Maria-Regina Kecht, ed., *Pedagogy Is Politics: Literary Theory and Critical Teaching* (Urbana: University of Illinois Press, 1992), p. 79. See also Roger I. Simon, "Forms of Insurgency in the Production of Popular Memories," in Henry A. Giroux and

Peter McLaren, eds., *Between Borders: Pedagogy and the Politics of Cultural Studies* (New York: Routledge, 1994).

18. A number of authors address Disney's imagined landscape as a place of economic and cultural power. See, for example, Zukin, *Landscapes of Power;* Michael Sorkin, "Disney World: The Power of Facade/the Facade of Power," in Sorkin, ed., *Variations on a Theme Park* (New York: Noonday, 1992); and see the especially impressive Stephen M. Fjellman, *Vinyl Leaves: Walt Disney World and America* (Boulder, Colo.: Westview, 1992).

19. In his brilliant book, Norman M. Klein argues that Disney constructed his expanded cartoons as a form of animated consumer memory. As Klein puts it, "The atmospheric lighting of Disney epic cartoons is very similar to the reverie of shopping, to shopping arcades, even to the permanent dusk of a room illuminated by television. It takes us more to the expanded shopping mall than a planned suburb, to a civilization based on consumer memories more than urban (or suburban) locations. . . . Disney showed us how to stop thinking of a city as residential or commercial, but rather as airbrushed streets in our mind's eye, a shopper's nonscape. If we can make a city remind us of animated consumer memory, it removes the alienation of changing cities, and replaces it with a cloud of imaginary store windows." *7 Minutes: The Life and Death of the American Animated Cartoon* (London: Verso, 1993, reprinted in 1998), p. 144.

20. The term "marketplace of culture" comes from Richard de Cordova, "The Mickey in Macy's Window: Childhood Consumerism and Disney Animation," in Eric Smoodin, ed., *Disney Discourse,* p. 209. Disney was one of the first companies to tie the selling of toys to the consuming of movies. Challenging the assumption that toy consumption was limited to seasonal sales, Disney actively created Mickey Mouse Clubs, advertised its toys in storefront windows, and linked its movies directly to the distribution of children's toys.

21. Richard Corliss, "The Mouse that Roars," *Time,* June 20, 1994, p. 59.

22. Richard Turner, "Walt Disney Presents: Forward to the Future," *Wall Street Journal,* August 26, 1994, p. B1.

23. Sallie Hofmeister, "In the Realm of Marketing, the 'Lion King' Rules," *New York Times,* July 12, 1994, p. D1.

24. Moira McCormick, " 'Hunchback' Soundtrack Tie-ins Abound," *Billboard,* May 25, 1996, p. 10.

25. Robert W. McChesney, *Corporate Media and the Threat to Democracy* (New York: Seven Stories Press, 1997), pp. 20–21.

26. For a summation of the merchandizing avalanche that accompanied the movie theater version of *The Lion King,* see Hofmeister, "In the Realm of Marketing."

27. Karen Schoemer, "An Endless Stream of Magic and Moola," *Newsweek,* September 5, 1994, p. 47.

28. Tom McNichol, "Pushing 'Pocahontas,' " *USA Weekend,* June 9–11, 1995, p. 4.

29. Tony Bennett touches on this issue through an explication of the concept of reading formation. He argues, "The concept of reading formation is an attempt to think of context as a set of discursive and inter-textual determinations, operating on material and institutional supports, which bear in upon a text not just externally, from the outside in, but internally, shaping it—in the historically concrete forms in which it is available as a text-to-be-read—from the inside out." "Texts in History: The Determinations of Readings and Their Texts," in Derek Atridge et al., eds., *Poststructuralism and the Question of History* (Cambridge: Cambridge University Press, 1987), p. 72.

30. Critiques of Disney's portrayal of girls and women can be found in Bell, Haas, and Sells, eds., *From Mouse to Mermaid*; Susan White, "Split Skins: Female Agency and Bodily Mutilation in *The Little Mermaid,*" in Jim Collins, Hilary Radner, and Ava Preacher Collins, eds., *Film Theory Goes to the Movies* (New York: Routledge, 1993), pp. 182–95.

31. Bonnie J. Leadbeater and Gloria Lodato Wilson, "Flipping Their Fins for a Place to Stand: 19th- and 20th-Century Mermaids," *Youth and Society* 27:4 (1993), pp. 466–86.

32. Susan Jefford, *Hard Bodies: Hollywood Masculinity in the Reagan Era* (New Brunswick: Rutgers University Press, 1994), p. 150.

33. Janet Maslin, "Disney Turns to a Warrior of the East in 'Mulan.' *New York Times,* June 19, 1998, p. B10.

34. I thank Valerie Janesick for this insight.

35. June Casagrande, "The Disney Agenda," *Creative Loafing,* March 17–23, 1994, pp. 6–7.

36. Upon its release in 1946, *Song of the South* was condemned by the National Association of the Advancement of Colored People for its racist representations.

37. For a historical context in which to understand Frontierland, see Fjellman, *Vinyl Leaves.*

38. These racist episodes are highlighted in Wiener, "Tall Tales and True."

39. Richard Scheinin, "Angry over 'Aladdin,'" *Washington Post,* January 10, 1993, p. G5.

40. Howard Green, a Disney spokesperson, dismissed the charges of racism as irrelevant, claiming that such criticisms were coming from a small minority and that "most people were happy" with the film. Scheinin, "Angry over Aladdin."

41. Jack Shaheen, "Animated Racism," *Cineaste* 20:1 (1993), p. 49.

42. Susan Miller and Greg Rode, "The Movie You See, the Movie You Don't: How Disney Do's that Old Time Derision," in Bell, Haas, and Sells, *From Mouse to Mermaid.*

43. Edward Said, *Culture and Imperialism* (New York: Knopf, 1993).

44. Susan Willis, "Fantasia: Walt Disney's Los Angeles Suite," *Diacritics* 17 (Summer 1987), pp. 83–96.

45. George Gerbner, Larry Gross, Michael Borgan, and Nancy Signorielli, "Growing Up with Television: The Cultivation Perspective," in Jennings Bryant and Dolf Zillmann, eds., *Media Effects: Advances in Theory and Research* (Hillsdale, N.J.: Erlbaum, 1995), p. 17.

46. See, for instance, Andrew Hart, ed., *Teaching the Media: International Perspectives* (Hillsdale, N.J.: Erlbaum, 1998).

47. David Buckingham, "Conclusion: Re-Reading Audiences," in David Buckingham, ed., *Reading Audiences: Young People and the*

Media (Manchester, U.K.: Manchester University Press, 1993), p. 211.

48. Cited in Zukin, *Landscapes of Power,* p. 222. While this quotation refers to Disney's view of its theme parks, it is an ideological view of history that shapes all of Disney's cultural productions. For a comment on how this view affects Disney's rendering of adult films, see Henry A. Giroux, *Disturbing Pleasures: Learning Popular Culture* (New York: Routledge, 1994), esp. pp. 25–45.

49. Fjellman, *Vinyl Leaves,* p. 400.

50. Rustom Bharacuha, "Around Ayodhya: Aberrations, Enigmas, and Moments of Violence," *Third Text,* no. 24 (Autumn 1993), p. 51.

51. Bennett, "Texts in History," p. 80.

52. Smoodin, "How to Read Walt Disney," pp. 4–5.

53. Mark Crispin Miller, "Free the Media," *Nation,* June 3, 1996, pp. 9–15.

54. For an example of such an analysis, see Stanley Aronowitz, *Roll over Beethoven* (Middletown: Wesleyan University Press, 1993); Giroux, *Disturbing Pleasures.*

55. Inderpal Grewal and Caren Kaplan, "Introduction: Transnational Feminist Practices and Questions of Postmodernity," in Inderpal Grewal and Caren Kaplan, eds., *Scattered Hegemonies* (Minneapolis: University of Minnesota Press, 1994).

MEMORY, NATION, AND FAMILY
IN DISNEY FILMS

An alarming defensiveness has crept into America's official image of itself, especially in its representations of the national past. Every society and official tradition defends itself against interferences with its sanctioned narratives; over time these acquire an almost theological status, with founding heroes, cherished ideas and values, national allegories having an inestimable effect in cultural and political life.

—Edward Said

INNOCENCE AND THE POLITICS OF MEMORY

There are few cultural icons in the United States that can match the signifying power of the Disney Company. Relentless in its efforts to promote a happy, kindly, paternal image of its founder, Walt Disney, and to send into the community an endless stream of representations and commodities that conjure up a nostalgic view of the United States as the "magic kingdom," the Disney Company has become synonymous with a notion of innocence that aggressively rewrites the historical and collective identity of the American past. Given their prominence in the construction of popular memory, Disney productions play an important but often overlooked role in the cultural battles over the present and future. Behind "the happiest place on earth" there is the institutional and ideological power of a multinational conglomerate that wields enormous social and political influence.

When politics is cloaked in the image of innocence, there is more at stake than simple deception. There is the issue of cultural power and how it influences public understandings of the past, national coherence, and popular memory in ways that often conceal injustice, criticism, and the possibility of democratic renewal.[1] Innocence, in Disney's world, becomes the ideological vehicle through which history is purged of its seamy side. In this case, innocence becomes important as an ideological construct less through its appeal to nostalgia, stylized consumption, or a unified notion of national identity than as a marker for recognizing the past as a terrain of pedagogical and ideological struggle. The Disney Company is not ignorant of history; it reinvents it as a pedagogical and political tool to secure its own interests.

Innocence is not only a rhetorical tool to legitimate dominant relations of power, it is also a pedagogical device that locates people in particular historical narratives, representations, and cultural practices. But before I discuss this "pedagogy of innocence," I want to define more specifically the central theoretical dimensions of pedagogy as a cultural politics and social practice. Needless to say, since the very meaning and purpose of pedagogy is constantly struggled over as a signifier, it is important to stress that the concept of pedagogy must be used with considerable discretion. There is no absolute sign under which pedagogy can be defined. Instead, pedagogy refers to the production of, and complex relationship among, knowledge, texts, desire, and identity; it signals how questions of audience, voice, power, and evaluation work to construct particular relations between teachers and students, institutions and society, and classrooms and communities.

In both conservative and progressive discourses, pedagogy is often treated simply as a set of strategies and skills to use to teach specified subject matter. In this context, pedagogy becomes synonymous with teaching as a technique, or the practice of a craft. Any viable notion of critical pedagogy must reject this one-sided definition and its imitations, even when they are claimed as part of a radical educational discourse or project.

Pedagogy in the more critical sense illuminates the relationship among knowledge, authority, and power. It draws attention to questions concerning who has control over the conditions for the production of knowledge. Moreover, it delineates the ways in which the circuit of power works through the various processes through which knowledge, identities, and authority are constructed within particular sets of social relations. In this case, critical pedagogy as a form of civic education refers to a deliberate attempt by cultural workers to influence how knowledge and subjectivities are produced within particular social relations. It draws attention to the ways in which knowledge, power, desire, and experience are produced under specific basic conditions of learning.

This approach to critical pedagogy does not reduce educational practice to the mastery of methodologies; it stresses, instead, the importance of understanding what actually happens in classrooms and other educational settings by raising questions regarding, in Roger Simon's words, "what knowledge is of most worth, in what direc-

tion should one desire, and what it means to know something."[2] Of course, the language of critical pedagogy does
something more. Pedagogy is simultaneously about the
knowledge and practices that teachers, parents, and students might engage in together and the cultural politics
and visions such practices legitimate. Finally, pedagogy is
not an a priori discourse or method but a context-specific,
theoretically informed practice that is the outcome of specific historical struggles over the power of educational practices to produce and valorize some identities while disa-
bling others. It is in this sense that cultural workers need
to be attentive to pedagogy as a political practice and the
cultural practices of pedagogy.

As a pedagogical construct that promotes a particular
view of history in Disney's diverse public cultures, innocence, when coupled with a mythic rendering of the past
and present, offers people the opportunity to envision
themselves as agents of history, as part of a community
longing for security and redemption in a world that often
seems hostile to such desires. Capitalizing on its inroads
into popular culture, Disney generates representations that
secure images, desires, and identifications through which
audiences come to produce themselves and negotiate their
relationships to others. By ordering and structuring such
representations, Disney mobilizes a notion of popular
memory that parades under the longing for childlike innocence, wholesome adventure, and frontier courage. Organized through affective and ideological forms of address,
such representations make particular claims upon the present and serve to define how, as Stuart Hall writes, we "come
to know how we are constituted and who we are."[3] What is
so important about the "wonderful world of Disney," as a
"historical-cultural theater of memory,"[4] is that it powerfully represents the degree to which, in Hall's words, "pop-

ular culture has historically become the dominant form of global culture . . . the scene, par excellence, of commodification, of the industries where culture enters directly into the circuits of . . . power and capital. It is the space of homogenization where stereotyping and the formulaic mercilessly process the material and experiences it draws into its web, where control over narratives and representations passes into the hands of established cultural bureaucracies, sometimes without a murmur."⁵

The strategies of escapism, historical forgetting, and repressive pedagogy in Disney's books, records, theme parks, movies, and TV programs produce identifications that define the United States as white, suburban, middle class, and heterosexual. Pedagogy, in Disney's diverse cultural texts, often functions as a history lesson that excludes the subversive elements of memory. Reduced to vignettes of childhood innocence, adventure, and chivalry, memory is removed from the historical, social, and political context, which defines memory as a process of cultural production that opens rather than closes down history. It is precisely this pedagogical policing of memory that undercuts it as a form of critical remembrance, which positions human agency between the possibilities of freedom and cultural largess, on the one hand, and the restrictions and boundaries set by the historical past, on the other.

For Disney, memory has nothing to do with remembering differently, nor is it a compelling force for arousing "dormant emancipatory energies . . . [and] intellectually satisfying and emotionally compelling political images."⁶ On the contrary, narrating the past becomes a vehicle for rationalizing the authoritarian, normalizing tendencies of the dominant culture that carry through to the present. Hence, Disney's pretense to innocence falls under the weight of a promotional culture predicated on the virtues of fun, family values, and, most important, consumption. The claim to high-spirited adventure and childlike innocence, albeit mischievous, in this case obscures a cultural universe that is largely conservative in its values, colonial in its production of racial differences, and middle class in its portrayal of family values. For example, Jane Kuenz and Susan Willis analyze how, in Disney's theme parks, intimacy, imagination, and spontaneity are replaced by the expertise of the well-placed park attendants, the picture-perfect photo sites, and the endless spectacles in which fun becomes consumption and memory is reduced to the purchase of souvenirs.[7] Similarly, theorists such as Ariel Dorfman and Armand Matellart indicate how Disney's comics inscribe sexist, racist, and colonial ideologies.[8]

Moreover, the mythology of an unproblematic innocence and clean virtue that has been carefully constructed by the Disney Company has been further demystified by revelations indicating that Walt Disney, because of his fervent anticommunism, developed a cordial relationship with the Federal Bureau of Investigation and its director, J. Edgar Hoover. Herbert Mitgang goes so far as to argue that "from 1940 until his death in 1966 [Walt Disney served] as a secret informer for the Los Angeles office of the Federal Bureau of Investigation."[9] Steven Watts modifies Mitgang's charge, arguing that at most Walt Disney "simply endorsed the agency's broader agenda of anti-communism during the tense days of the Cold War."[10] But Watts also underplays the fact that Walt was appointed special FBI agent (code name, S.A.C. Contact) and that he was far from innocent in his dedication to rooting out communist agitators in the film industry. Moreover, Walt also allowed the FBI access to Disneyland facilities for "use in connection with official matters for recreational purposes."[11] Walt also granted J. Edgar Hoover the opportunity to censor and modify the scripts of Disney films such as *Moon Pilot* (1962) and *That Darn Cat* (1965), which included harmless satires of the FBI.

The policing of memory erases the emancipatory possibilities of memory, as illuminated by public revelations that the Disney Company has on occasion prevented the publication of books critical of Walt Disney and the Disney Company.[12] Behind the magical name of Disney and the public spaces it represents lurks the power of a multinational conglomerate that has little regard for free speech and public criticism.

MEMORY, POLITICS, AND IDENTITY

Disney films inscribe the link between the related issues of memory, politics, and identity. In what follows, I analyze the films *Good Morning, Vietnam* (1987) and *Pretty Woman* (1990) as exemplary texts for engaging the terrain of popular culture as it is constructed within the discourse of innocence and "fun," which lies at the heart of the Disney Company's worldview.[13] Although these films were made in the late 1980s and early 1990s, they are important ideological markers in linking the pedagogical and the political because of the claims they make on our understanding of the past, because of the "changing attitudes and ambivalence concerning women's autonomy and sexuality, as well as values associated with class differences."[14]

Good Morning, Vietnam exemplifies Hollywood's attempts throughout the nineties to depoliticize the democratic impulses of the sixties by rewriting the period as one of sexual debauchery, drug-induced hysteria, and moral decadence. In many ways, *Good Morning, Vietnam* provides the backdrop for one of the most successful and reactionary films on the sixties produced in the nineties: *Forrest Gump* (1994). Similarly, *Pretty Woman* foregrounds and legitimates Disney's hostility to feminism by seizing upon the backlash that had begun to gain momentum in the beginning of the nineties, while offering a pseudofeminism grounded in the traditional Disney take on family values.[15] It should come as no surprise that Disney would recycle, in the late 1990s, *The Parent Trap*, a film that embraces a notion of family values that reads as a script for a 1950s version of *Ozzie and Harriet.*

Yet, although not produced for children, both *Good Morning, Vietnam* and *Pretty Woman* project the same insidious ethos of childhood innocence the Disney Company enforces in many of its products. In different ways, both films demonstrate how the discourse of patriarchy, class, and sexism are couched in the language and representations of innocence and how such representations mobilize popular memory to incorporate a politics of forgetting in producing a particular view of class relations, consumerism, patriarchy, and family values. I focus here on the film *Good Morning, Vietnam* because I believe it is one of the most important films Disney has produced in its attempt to render the way in which a major historical event is remembered and understood. But more important, *Good Morning, Vietnam* provides a particularly compelling case for understanding how Disney uses the images and representations of popular culture as part of a pedagogical process that makes an "educational claim on the past . . . so that it can make a difference in the present."[16]

In addition, Disney's ideology has been analyzed largely through critiques of its theme parks and comics and seldom through its films (Walt Disney, Touchstone, Miramax, and Hollywood Pictures), nor have these critiques used pedagogical criticism to analyze Disney's texts as ideologi-

cal narratives. Pedagogical critiques of Disney films are war-
ranted on two counts: first, the films construct and reach a
much wider audience than Disney's other cultural enterprises; second, the films have enormous value as popular
texts, since they are readily available for pedagogical and
cultural criticism.

THE WAR OF LAUGHTER AND FORGETTING

It has become a commonplace that the Vietnam War represents a watershed in United States history. Marked by
widespread popular protest against American colonialism,
the war demythologized the role of the United States as a
world leader; it mobilized diverse movements of resistance
and revealed a deep-seated racism that structured policies
toward both minorities at home and people of color outside our national boundaries. Moreover, this was a postmodern war, a media event that signaled the limits of conventional warfare and the power of American militarism
and imperialism while simultaneously transforming the
horror and violence of war into a television spectacle. The
Vietnam conflict signaled not simply the death of "truth"
but also what Theodor Adorno calls in another context
"the withering of experience" and, hence, the displace-
ment of the imperatives of moral responsibility and human
agency:

> The total obliteration of the war by information, propa-
> ganda, commentaries, with cameramen in their first tanks
> and war reporters dying heroic deaths, the mishmash of an
> enlightened manipulation of public opinion and oblivious
> activity: all this is another expression for the withering of
> experience, the vacuum between men and their fate, in
> which their real fate lies. It is as if the reified, hardened plas-

ter-cast of events takes the place of events themselves. Men are reduced to walk-on parts in a monster documentary-film.[17]

In the 1970s and 1980s, the rewriting of the United States intervention in Vietnam became the focus of celluloid history. Vietnam as a spectacle provided the impetus for a series of Hollywood films engaged in the process of organized forgetting, a process that substituted myths for reality, redemption for truth, and collective self-pity for social justice.

With few exceptions, Hollywood's rendition of the Vietnam War paralleled and legitimated the nation's colonial strategy in Southeast Asia. It shifted the focus of the war away from the victims of long-standing Western, specifically North American, imperialism to the personal and social struggles of Americans involved in the war. The legacy of historical amnesia during the 1980s and the construction of popular memory in Hollywood Vietnam films is well known and need not be repeated here.[18] After all, this was the decade in which the United States needed to reassert itself as the leader of the "new world order" by exorcising the legacy of the 1960s and reversing the public humiliation it suffered during the Iran hostage crisis. At the same time, the United States was actively obscuring and erasing its own legacy of military intervention and terrorism in world affairs by constructing Third World peoples as either terrorists or religious fundamentalists.

It is impossible to separate the critical acclaim and popular success of *Good Morning, Vietnam* from the context and content of Vietnam films that preceded it. Directed by Barry Levinson, written by Mitch Markowitz, and produced by Walt Disney Touchstone Pictures, *Good Morning, Vietnam* appealed to a generation of youth whose knowledge of the Vietnam War comes from the electronic media. This is a generation twice removed from the moral and political issues that surrounded the Vietnam conflict. In fact, David Butler, the author of *The Fall of Saigon,* revealed to a *New York Times* reporter that one of the key elements in making the film was "the coming [of age] of a younger audience for whom the war is less controversial." According to Butler, "Vietnam intrigues the yuppie generation but it doesn't torture them."[19] Barry Levinson, the director of the film, supports this position through his own experience of the Vietnam conflict. While working at a television station in the late 1960s, Levinson claims he learned about Vietnam by watching daily footage come in over the CBS feed (although it is hard to discern what he learned, since he claims that he didn't understand what the war was about).[20]

In addition to the emergence of a new generation of moviegoers and a director with no political and personal commitment to the Vietnam War, the third major factor structuring the context of this film was the role it provided for Robin Williams to exercise the full range of his comic, manic improvisations. This is borne out not simply by the many reviews of the film that focus almost exclusively on Williams but also by the remarks of Jeffrey Katzenberg, chairman of Walt Disney Studios at the time: *Good Morning, Vietnam,* he said, was appealing because it gave Williams's comic talent its full range.[21]

What separates *Good Morning, Vietnam* from other Vietnam films is its unabashed refusal to engage the Vietnam conflict through the traditional tropes of homelessness, revenge, and patriotism. Instead, *Good Morning, Vietnam* willfully expunges the discourses of history, politics, and ethics from its narrative to appeal to a generation of youth raised on the affective energies of high-tech rock, 1980s yuppie buffoonery, and a narcissistic assertion of whiteness as the single referent for intelligence, manhood, and sensuality. In this instance, a Reagan-era-inspired slapstick conception of the world functions to license a reactionary view of the war that substitutes spectacle for critical engagement. But there is more at work in this film than the specter of U.S. military aggression hiding behind the legacy of happy times that informed the propaganda machine of the Reagan/Bush administrations. It is precisely because of its facile dismissal of politics and history that *Good Morning, Vietnam* unwittingly lays bare, through its omissions and self-righteous moralism, its complicity with the broader discourse of Western colonialism.

Good Morning, Vietnam takes place in Saigon in 1965. The film is a partly fictionalized comedy drama about an army disc jockey, Adrian Cronauer, played by Robin Williams, who is sent to Vietnam to beef up the morale of the troops at a point when the military conflict is beginning its steep escalation. Cronauer arrives with two weapons in his personal arsenal: his iconoclastic style and his manic wit. With these, he immediately breathes new life into the American Armed Forces radio station. Cronauer's short-lived sojourn in Saigon constitutes the heart of the film and parallels that period of the Vietnam conflict marked by an increase in antiwar sentiments at home and the escalation of military aggression against the Vietnamese people.

Cronauer first appears in Saigon as an irrepressible motormouth, who combines the style of the 1960s counterculture with the comic wit of an irreverent Bob Hope. Waiting to meet Cronauer at the Saigon military airport is Edward Garlick, an African American soldier played by Forest Whitaker. Garlick is one of the few blacks to appear in the film; he is a shuffling, clumsy grunt whose only missions in life are to laugh indiscriminately at all of Cronauer's jokes and to be his dutiful servant. Within the first minute of the film, Cronauer rattles off five jokes and insults Garlick by telling him to get a new name and learn how to drive a jeep. Removing any doubt about his role as the colonial master, Cronauer allows Garlick to serve as his "domestic" tour guide, ordering him to pursue various Vietnamese women so that Cronauer can sexually harass them while being driven to the military base.

Cronauer's arrival and his drive to the base set up one of the primary structuring principles of the film. Humor not only serves to position the identity of Vietnamese women as merely Western sexual commodities, it also links the objectification of the Vietnamese to the internal colonialism that Cronauer reproduces in his relationship with Garlick. But Cronauer's racism, sexism, and belief in the moral rightness of the war is neither framed in nor tempered by the realism of earlier Vietnam films. Instead, they are couched in daily routines and actions that simply provide fodder for Cronauer's incessant one-line jokes. Grounded in comic routines, Cronauer's reference to the Vietnamese as "little people" and his claim that the Vietnamese women have "behinds designed by a Jewish scientist in Switzerland" position the audience to indulge their own complicity with such racism and sexism without having to be morally responsible for it.

But because his actions are grounded in comedy, Cronauer still personifies all of the "sweetness and goodness" typical of Disney characters. Besieged on all fronts, he moves between the irreverence of Donald Duck and the gritty humanism of Dick Tracy. The first display of Cronauer's resistance appears early in the film over the choice of music that is to be aired on the radio station. Confronted by his immediate army superiors, whose musical taste was shaped in the 1940s and is totally out of touch with the

musical interests of the troops, Cronauer ditches the Man-
tovani/Percy Faith–style programming and unleashes a bar-
rage of rock 'n' roll music accompanied by satirical jokes.
To the dismay of his commanding officers, Cronauer's
radio show becomes a big hit among the troops, and Cronauer himself begins to emerge as a popular, controversial
figure in Saigon. By stressing the subversive qualities of
rock 'n' roll and popular culture, the film constructs one of
the three major conflicts that will serve to define the Dis-
ney/Levinson view of the war.

In the first instance, the struggle over popular music suggests that the war was primarily a generational conflict between teenage soldiers reared on the rock 'n' roll of James
Brown, Martha and the Vandellas, and Wayne Fontana and
the military leadership, with its out-of-touch middlebrow
musical taste. But the use of rock 'n' roll music in this film
also serves to transform the politics of the war into a stylized aesthetics that renders the presence of the American
troops in terms fashioned from a tourist magazine. With
few exceptions, the voice-over music is played against images of American soldiers playing volleyball, lounging on
boats, and casually walking in the streets of Saigon. One
gets the impression that the soldiers are holiday visitors
flooding the local economy with their goodwill and buying
power or that, when on duty, they mostly hang out listen-
ing to the radio. As the champion of popular culture, Cronauer combines a touch of MTV hipness with a traditional
dose of upbeat patriotism. Iconoclasm links, in this case, a
depoliticized form of resistance with the highly political
task of attempting to boost the morale of soldiers intent on
"exterminating the enemy."

Another conflict facing Cronauer is military news censorship. After a terrorist bombing of Jimmy Wah's, a popular Saigon nightclub, Cronauer defies his commanding of-

ficer and reports the incident in his news broadcast. But what might have emerged as an insight into the role of the media, the government, and the army in distorting the information given to the public about the war is, instead, a narrative of Cronauer's self-pity. Suspended from his job, Cronauer offers neither critical insight into the broader reasons behind his dismissal nor any resistance to his fate. Instead, he soothes his wounded ego by hanging out in Saigon bars, fraternizing with Vietnamese nationals, and telling jokes to anyone who will listen. By privatizing the issue of media censorship, Disney/Levinson erase any reference to the historic conditions that necessitated such censorship in the first place and shift the terrain of anguish and suffering away from the massive devastation being visited upon the Vietnamese people. In the end, the audience is positioned to sympathize with the problems of a disgruntled middle-class white man who also happens to be actively complicitous with a military machine that, according to John Pilger, "dropped the greatest tonnage of bombs in the history of warfare—half a ton of explosives for every man, woman, and child" in Vietnam.[22]

The third conflict that structures the film concerns Cronauer's relationship with "otherness"; that is, those Vietnamese men and women who inhabit the landscape outside of Cronauer's radio station. Soon after Cronauer arrives in Vietnam, he accosts and then follows a Vietnamese woman to an English class for Vietnamese civilians. He bribes the army officer teaching the class to allow him to take it over so he can meet the woman he has followed. Using the class as the vehicle for a comedy routine, Cronauer attempts to teach English through the nuances of street-corner American slang. This is a significant moment in the film not merely because of its unabashed portrayal of Vietnamese women as simply objects of a white American male's sexual desire but also because it further denies the cultural specificity of the linguistic and historical setting that Cronauer inhabits. After all, why should Vietnamese nationals be learning English? And why should they be learning American slang taught by a white man talking as if he were a working-class black? But, more important, it is the refusal to recognize that the Vietnamese themselves have their own language, culture, and history. English has a long tradition of being the linguistic face of colonialism, and that tradition is reinforced rather than disrupted in this film.

At the end of the class, Cronauer is confronted by the Vietnamese woman's brother, Tran, who tells him to keep away from his sister. Tran is quite clear about Cronauer's motives and describes him as simply another colonialist trying to buy his way into the culture. Cronauer ignores the comment and attempts to befriend him by taking him to a local nightclub. While at Jimmy Wah's club, Tran is confronted by racist GIs, who insult him and try to throw him out of the bar. Cronauer, once again, occupies center stage and, in attempting to defend Tran, initiates a full-fledged brawl. Amazingly, Tran then becomes his Vietnamese friend and sidekick. Functioning as a devoted guide, Tran saves Cronauer from Jimmy Wah's nightclub minutes before it is blown up by the Vietcong. He arranges for Cronauer to visit his village, and he eventually saves Cronauer's life by rescuing him from a Vietcong patrol that has blown up his jeep and is searching for him in the jungle outside of Saigon. What is startling about Tran's character is, that near the end of *Good Morning, Vietnam,* it is revealed that he is a Vietcong terrorist!

Tran's character is significant because it combines a dual reading and interpretation, one that is both racist and colonial. In the first instance, Tran embodies the long history of racial stereotypes that permeate hegemonic versions of popular culture in the United States.[23] More specifically, Tran's character and relationship to Cronauer exemplify the use of racial representations to designate "otherness" as an embodiment of infantilism, as a signifier for excluding those who do not belong to the national community. In this representation, Tran is denied any significant human presence. Instead, he is presented through a dominant fantasy, which reduces the "other" to an object of pleasure and servitude. Like Garlick, Tran is the Vietnamese version of Tonto, serving his colonial master obediently and generously. Within such representations, Tran is denied any sense of agency that would problematize the American military presence in Vietnam. Within what Judith Butler calls this "racially saturated field of visibility,"[24] Tran becomes simply another "gook," who is both marginal and irrelevant to viewers' understanding of the political and historical nature of the Vietnam War. Commenting on the use of such representations in American literature, Toni Morrison says, "Cooperative or sullen, they are Tontos all, whose role is to do everything possible to serve the Lone Ranger without disturbing his indulgent delusion that he is indeed alone."[25]

But Tran's representation is twofold. Not only is he the Hollywood version of Tonto, he is also a Vietcong terrorist. Shocked by the revelation that his trusted friend is in real life a member of the Vietnamese resistance, Cronauer searches out Tran and castigates him for betraying their friendship and trust. Revealing Tran as a Vietcong and terrorist also fuels a racial mistrust of those "others" who, according to a long-standing racial code, appear to be one's friend but in the end can never be trusted. Embodying the myth of both the solitary hero and the righteous, puritanical American, Cronauer employs the language of humanism to highlight his own angst and to position Tran (and all Vietnamese resistance fighters) as criminal and terrorist. Mobilizing all of the courtroom drama that has been played out within the last decade in the public press over the Rodney King and O. J. Simpson trials as well as over the courtroom spectacles surrounding the prosecution of various high-profile black rap artists, *Good Morning, Vietnam* presents criminality and lawlessness as a racial category. In this instance, Tran symbolizes all those "others" who jeopardize American national unity and threaten Western culture and civility.

If Tran is the colonial "other," Tran's sister, Tuan, is nearly invisible except as an object of lust. Though she refuses to date Cronauer, her identity is completely constructed within his patriarchal gaze. Her refusal is expressed as a form of resistance not to American imperialism or to the relentless assaults of Cronauer's sexism but to the Vietnamese custom of civility. Tuan refuses to become romantically involved with him because her family and community frown on such behavior by Vietnamese women. When Cronauer is about to leave Saigon, he meets with her and his class of students one last time. As a parting gesture, he engages in a game of American baseball with the students and appears forlorn that he could not consummate his romantic fantasies. Tuan also smiles, indicating that, if it weren't for the war, they would be able to indulge their repressed passions. In this instance, Tuan is portrayed as a tragic character who has to repress her desires because of the inconvenience of the war.

Tuan is nothing more than a stick figure, a Barbie doll who merely testifies to the frustration, heterosexuality, and virility of the lonely American hero, further reinforcing and legitimating the eroticization of Vietnamese women and the dependence of many of these women on prostitution in order to survive during the war. At the conclusion of the film, there is an extraordinary display of Disney sentimentality when Cronauer's English class thanks him for teaching them English and Tuan thanks him for being so kind!

There are two related but important scenes that frame the conclusion of *Good Morning, Vietnam.* As Cronauer is being driven to the airfield, the camera focuses on the new recruits entering Saigon. On one level, this is an obvious comment on the escalation of the war that took place in 1965. On a less obvious level, it expresses the deeply racist nature of this film. Almost all of the recruits are white and appear to be largely middle class. This is an amazing misrepresentation, given that a disproportionate number of soldiers who fought in Vietnam were poor, were high school dropouts, and were African American or Latino. As Cronauer is about to catch his plane, he says to Garlick, "Carry on, Montesquieu." True to the colonialism of the film, Garlick replies, "I like that, it makes me feel British."

Good Morning, Vietnam does more than produce racial and colonial representations. It erases any sense of collective agency or responsibility and builds its narrative structure around the emotional experiences of the isolated, alienated American resister. Moreover, it redefines resistance in terms that are apolitical and ahistorical. Completely missing from this film is any indication that there was a massive antiwar movement in the United States, that an enormous number of soldiers opposed the war, and that it was colonial and racist policies that produced this resistance.

WORKING-CLASS WOMEN AND THE DISNEY IDEA OF FAMILY

Popular memory and the discourse of innocence in Disney's films are not limited to reasserting dominant versions of national identity, nor do these films attempt to fashion such a discourse in isolation from other ideological considerations. Cultural identities are also produced and consumed through Disney's aggressive attempts, as David Morely and Kevin Robins put it, to "articulate the private and public spheres: to connect the family and the nation."[26] The pervasive symbol of ideological unification through which Disney defines its view of capitalism, gender, and national identity is the family, more particularly, the white, nuclear, middle-class family.

This family becomes the ethical referent for linking consumerism, gender roles, motherhood, and class chivalry, and it is around this family (as the primary unit of stability, culture, ethics, and agency) that Disney weaves, in many of its films, the articulating principle that links "individuals and their families to the centers of national life, offering the audience an image of itself and of the nation as a knowable community, a wider public world beyond the routines of a narrow existence."[27] Disney's attempt to structure issues of gender and class around family values is especially evident in one of its most financially lucrative films, *Pretty Woman*.

Directed by Garry Marshall, *Pretty Woman*, on the one hand, is a contemporary rewrite of the Pygmalion and Cinderella classics. Innocence triumphs over adversity when the down-and-out, though not unvirtuous, working-class prostitute, Vivian (played by Julia Roberts), steps into a dream world by meeting, seducing, saving, and then marrying the rich corporate raider, Edward Lewis, played by Richard Gere. On another level, *Pretty Woman* signifies Disney's attempt to renegotiate the relationship between the new patriarchy (i.e., the sensitive man) and the modern "single woman" of the 1980s and 1990s and to rationalize this relationship with the logic of the marketplace and traditional family values. In this attempt to renegotiate the relationship between patriarchal power and the agency of the "new" woman, Touchstone Pictures reveals its political strategy and ideological imperatives. That is, the company demonstrates its willingness to struggle over popular culture by adjusting its ideological weapons to the shifting assumptions and practices that characterize the changing roles and conceptions of work, consumption, and identity that men and women are experiencing in what might be termed a post-Fordist society.[28]

In general terms, the story revolves around the improbable courtship of Edward and Vivian. Edward is a charming corporate thug who buys companies, breaks them up, and then sells off the various parts for enormous profits. Vivian is a Disney version of the child-woman, who has left her family only to find herself lost and desperate in the big city, reduced to prostituting herself on the street. Both characters have fallen from grace in this Disney narrative, and both are given the status of the tragic hero. Edward's masculinity is embodied in a rapacious capitalist desire to control property, companies, and women. But it is not patriarchal desire that is subject to criticism in *Pretty Woman*. On the contrary, Edward's need to position Vivian as his "beck and call girl," ready to fulfill his every desire, is used as a cinematic device to give Vivian the opportunity to become an agent of her own sexual and consumer desires. Disney's version of patriarchy is used to expand the agency of women into the public sphere of the marketplace.

Edward's patriarchal obsessions are not the focus of criticism in *Pretty Woman*: rather, it is the ruthlessness he employs in the buying and selling of companies. But in the innocent world of Disney, such ruthlessness is presented not as a systemic feature of capitalism but as a psychological problem resulting from the breakdown of traditional values in Edward's own family. In a revealing conversation with Vivian, Edward tells her that his father left his mother for another woman. Along with his infidelity, Edward's father also made off with all of the family wealth. Edward's mother died soon afterward, leaving Edward angry and unsettled over his father's destruction of the family. Adding a theoretical twist to the idea that the marketplace can provide effective therapy, Edward exhibits a new Oedipal turn by destroying his father's company through a corporate buyout that he personally oversees. In this instance, Edward combines corporate greed and personal vengeance, adding a therapeutic advantage to the practice of corporate sleaze.

Written as a narrative of investment and return, the cultural and material capital at work in *Pretty Woman* celebrates Edward's willingness to invest in a woman who is also bereft of the regulating laws of the traditional family. Edward's "generosity" and business acumen gain for him the benefits of Vivian's sexual expertise, while simultaneously creating the conditions for Vivian's own sense of agency. In Disney's terms, the agency of women outside of the traditional family is reduced to the freedom to buy expensive clothing and to reinvent their identities within the logic and terms of white, middle-class cultural capital. As Hilary Radner notes, Vivian's "transformation from prostitute to woman of privilege is effected solely through her ability to purchase and wear fashionable garments—to 'look good' in fashionable clothing. This is her most obvious skill, the necessary complement to her willing expertise in the bedroom."[29] Patriarchy, in this instance, becomes the vehicle through which Edward becomes a born-again capitalist. Vivian redeems her identity through her consumer practices.[30]

In the end, both Vivian and Edward throw off the psychological baggage they carry as the result of the loss or the abandonment of the family and reestablish the promise and viability of marriage and the middle-class, heterosexual family as a vehicle for upward mobility and for the moral redemption of the humanist, capitalist subject. Of course, beneath the play of innocence redeemed in *Pretty Woman* lies the violent erasure of avarice and sexism that links capitalism, consumerism, and patriarchy in Disney's world.

In the final scene of *Pretty Woman,* Edward has his black chauffeur drive him to Vivian's apartment, where he rescues her from a life of destitution. In one of the final shots, the camera pans back to the street from Vivian's apartment and frames the black chauffeur standing next to a white stretch Cadillac. Like Garlick and so many other black characters in Disney films, he appears ecstatic that he can share in the white characters' joy, in this case the result of the merger of Edward's capital and Vivian's body. It is precisely this colonial signifier of whiteness, power, and degradation that reveals the racist ideology underlying *Pretty Woman.* This is a film for men whose desire for wealth can now be mediated by the "new woman," who will "bring [them] back to the fold of a capitalism regulated by the law of the family and patriarchal responsibility."³¹ In this film, white men constitute the source of all authority; women provide sexual pleasures and the potential for new markets; and people of color and working-class people "dream" about the possibilities of upward mobility.

MEMORY AND THE PEDAGOGIES OF POWER

Good Morning, Vietnam and *Pretty Woman* are exemplary cultural texts because they offer the potential for a critical reading of how the politics of innocence works to conceal the ideological principles used to legitimate a racist conception of global imperialism, a nostalgic sense of history, and a dominant assertion of family values. As popular culture texts, these films function through discursive and ideological practices that are both pedagogical and political. As part of a larger cultural apparatus, they signify the centrality of film as a medium of popular culture, a centrality that must be addressed not simply as a pedagogical apparatus actively involved in diverse identity formations but also for the crucial role it plays in the construction of national identities in the service of global expansion and colonialism.

Educators, parents, students, and other cultural workers need to redefine the relationship between the political and the pedagogical and to produce alternative approaches to mass culture. Otherwise, the mobilization of popular memory by the dominant culture will continue to enable "cultural institutions and cultural arbiters to present their histories as seamless, disinterested, and authoritative, and their hierarchies of value as universally valid, ecumenical, and effectively consensual."[32]

Progressives, recognizing that cultural texts such as *Good Morning, Vietnam* and *Pretty Woman* mobilize social and popular memories to legitimate particular versions of the past, need to expand their understanding of the sites where a pedagogy of power is used to produce particular narratives about who is authorized to speak, under what conditions, and in whose interest. Since we live in an age that borders on a crisis of forgetting, it is all the more imperative to expand the boundaries of the political to encompass not merely formerly marginalized cultural practices but also a new politics of representation.[33]

At the very least, such a politics would require, as Roger Simon points out, a consideration of all those pedagogical sites in which the past is being constructed as crucial locations of struggle.[34] This suggests extending the meaning and practice of pedagogy far beyond schools. Furthermore, it suggests redefining how cultural politics can be understood beyond the often highly guarded boundaries of single-issue considerations and identity politics. This is both a call for a hybridized politics and a recognition that questions concerning the relationship between authority and power must address who has control over the conditions necessary for the production of knowledge. At stake here are questions of access, political economy, and a representational politics that lays bare its own practices in relation to the dominant relations of cultural, material, and social production.

By erasing the political and ethical considerations that make history a site of struggle, Disney has produced a filmic version of popular culture through a pedagogy that rewrites history as inheritance and human agency as a condition for adapting to injustice. Electronically mediated images, especially television and film, represent one of the most potent arms of cultural hegemony in the twenty-first century. Constituted as a public sphere with an enormous global reach, the power of the electronic media reinforces the widely held assumption that there is no politics outside of representation.

But if progressive cultural workers are to take such a politics seriously, they must use pedagogy as an articulating category to unravel how they might actively share in developing alternative conditions for giving people ownership over the control and production of knowledge and authority in the service of a radical democratic politics. The influential pedagogues of the twentieth century are not simply the hard-working teachers of the public school system; they are also the dominant cultural agents who mediate the public cultures of advertising, radio talk shows, the malls, and the cinema multiplexes. It is in these representational domains, fashioned through powerful forms of address, that the intersection of unmet needs and the mundane desires of daily life are made concrete. Within these public cultures people both identify and lose themselves in representations that bring them the promise of hope or, more likely, the swindle of fulfillment.

The challenge of a new cultural politics, one that takes popular and media culture seriously, is as much a pedagogical challenge as a political one. The issue for cultural workers is (1) to recognize the importance of cultural texts such as *Good Morning, Vietnam* and *Pretty Woman* in shaping social identities and (2) to address how representations are constructed through social memories, which are taught, learned, mediated, and appropriated within particular institutional and discursive formations of power. Any social movement, regardless of how theoretically enlightened it may be, that ignores this issue runs the risk of reproducing a politics that is both silent about its own pedagogical visions and unresponsive to how the culture industry contains dissent and overwhelms democracy in the name of a self-serving appeal to entertainment.

Disney's construction of historical memory, innocence, and family values points beyond the past while remaining firmly within it. Disney culture offers a certain notion of history that is not only safe and middle class but also indifferent to racial, class, and social conflict. As distorted as Disney's dreamscape might be, it contains a utopian element in that it offers an antidote to the boredom, brutality, and estrangement that appear to be such a pervasive part of daily life. To condemn Disney while simultaneously affirming the unhappy consciousness of powerlessness and despair is to reaffirm the very conditions that make Disney so appealing to those who want to escape from a culture in which cynicism has become a permanent fixture.

Democratic public life needs to be informed by utopian traces that allow us to venture beyond the present in order to salvage as much as possible from those desires that link the past to an anticipation of a better life, a life built upon the precepts of compassion and justice rather than distorted by images of fantasy, nostalgia, and a longing for insularity that embody the inverted hopes and dreams offered by the narrow visions of Disney's corporate culture and the logic of the market.

NOTES

1. On the issue of memory and politics, I am indebted to these writings: Roger I. Simon, "Forms of Insurgency in the Production of Popular Memories," in Henry A. Giroux and Peter McLaren, eds., *Between Borders: Pedagogy and the Politics of Cultural Studies* (New York: Routledge, 1994); Harvey Kaye, *The Powers of the Past* (Minneapolis: University of Minnesota Press, 1991); Yose Hayim Yerushalmi, *Zakhor: Jewish History and Jewish Memory* (New York: Schocken, 1989); James E. Young, *The Texture of Memory* (New Haven: Yale University Press, 1993); Geoffrey Hartman, "Public Memory and Its Discontents," *Raritan* 8:4 (1984), pp. 24–40; Marita Sturken, *Tangled Memories* (Berkeley: University of California Press, 1997).

2. Roger I. Simon, "For a Pedagogy of Possibility," *Critical Pedagogy Networker* 1:1 (1988), p. 2.

3. Stuart Hall, "What Is the 'Black' in Popular Culture?" in Gina Dent, ed., *Black Popular Culture* (Seattle: Bay Press, 1992), p. 30.

4. James Clifford, "On Collecting Art and Culture," in Russell Ferguson, Martha Gever, Trinh T. Minh-ha, and Cornel West, eds., *Out There: Marginalization and Contemporary Cultures* (Cambridge: MIT Press, 1990), p. 164.

5. Hall, "What Is the 'Black' in Popular Culture?" p. 26.

6. Walter Adamson, *Marx and the Disillusionment of Marxism* (Berkeley: University of California Press, 1984), p. 238.

7. See Jane Kuenz, "It's a Small World After All: Disney and the Pleasures of Identification," *South Atlantic Quarterly* 92:1 (1993), pp. 63–88; Susan Willis, "Disney World: Public Use/Private State," *South Atlantic Quarterly* 92: 1 (1993), pp. 119–37.

8. Ariel Dorfman and Armand Mattelart, *How to Read Donald Duck: Imperialist Ideology in the Disney Comic* (New York: International General Editions, 1975).

9. Herbert Mitgang, "Disney Link to the F.B.I. and Hoover Is Disclosed," *New York Times,* May 6, 1993, p. B1.

10. Steven Watts, *The Magic Kingdom: Walt Disney and the American Way of Life* (New York: Houghton Mifflin, 1998), p. 327.

11. Mitgang, "Disney Link to the F.B.I.," p. B4.

12. See Weiner's comments on the Disney Company's involvement in preventing Marc Eliot's book, *Walt Disney: Hollywood's Dark Prince,* from being published by Bantam in 1991. Jon Weiner, "Murdered Ink," *Nation,* May 31, 1993, p. 743.

13. The way in which Disney erases serious historical, political, social, and economic issues by appealing to sentimental posturing, personal anguish, comic irony, and the virtues of generous patriarchy can be seen in the rampant sexism and ruthless attack on single, working-class mothers in *Stella* (1990); the right-wing nativism of *Green Card* (1990); the celebration of consumerism in *Scenes from a Mall* (1991); the capitalist principles in organized crime in *Billy Bathgate* (1991); the superficial humanist appeal to the virtues of medical research in *Medicine Man* (1992); the "comic" and historically banal portrayal of working-class youth in *Newsies* (1992); the blatant consumerist manipulation in *Hercules* (1997) (represented by transforming *Hercules* into a blatant advertisement for kids to visit a Disney Store); and more recently, the appeal to traditional family values in the remake of *The Parent Trap* (1998).

14. D. Soyini Madison, "*Pretty Woman* through the Triple Lens of Black Feminist Spectatorship," in Elizabeth Bell, Lynda Haas,

and Laura Sells, eds., *From Mouse to Mermaid* (Bloomington: Indiana University Press, 1995), p. 225.

15. See Susan Faludi, *Backlash* (New York: Crown, 1991).

16. Simon, "Forms of Insurgency," p. 131.

17. Theodor Adorno, *Minima Moralia: Reflections from a Damaged Life,* translated by E. F. N. Jephcott (London: New Left Books, 1974), p. 55.

18. Hollywood blockbusters such as *Rolling Thunder* (1977), *Coming Home* (1978), *The Deer Hunter* (1978), *First Blood* (1982), and *Born on the Fourth of July* (1990) focus on the plight of returning veterans, their personal reactions to the war, and their readjustment to a society that appeared to reject them. In these films, the war is brought home while subverting any substantive political and moral commentary on the war itself. The legacy of the Vietnam conflict is either displaced through a focus on the subjective experiences of veterans or, in the case of the Rambo films, viewed as an expression of individual corruption and political ineptness on the part of U.S. government officials.

In the 1980s, films such as *Platoon* (1986), *Gardens of Stone* (1987), *Full Metal Jacket* (1987), and *Hamburger Hill* (1987) initiated another round of mythologizing. Reduced to the existential struggles and narratives of actual combat troops, the Vietnam War was rewritten as a coming-of-age tale. The war in these scenarios is a dehumanizing and traumatizing event, but it is framed by a liberal and narrowly defined humanist focus on individual suffering.

At the height of the Reagan era, Hollywood rewrote the Vietnam War in the image of an unbridled and arrogant national machismo. Films such as *Uncommon Valor* (1983), *Missing in Action* (1984), *Missing in Action, 2: The Beginning* (1985), *Rambo: First Blood, Part II* (1985), and *The Hanoi Hilton* (1987) used Vietnam as a backdrop to celebrate heroic rescues. Chemical warfare, forced settlements, and the burning of villages on the part of the U.S. military were written out of history, as Hollywood invented wooden macho men intent on saving the real victims of Vietnam, the MIAs, from the demonized Vietnamese. At stake in this version of popular memory was not the expurgation of collective guilt but the construction of a vision of masculinity that resonated with the conservative image of national identity and patriotism that informed the Reagan years. A superb anthology on Hollywood films and the Vietnam War is Linda Dittmar and Gene Michard, eds., *From Hanoi to Hollywood: The Vietnam War in American Film* (New Brunswick: Rutgers University Press, 1990). For two exceptional critiques of Vietnam War films, see John Pilger, "Vietnam, Another Hollywood Fairy Story," *Guardian,* March 10, 1990, pp. 22–23; and J. Hoberman, "Vietnam: The Remake," in Barbara Kruger and Phil Mariani, eds., *Remaking History* (Seattle: Bay Press, 1989), pp. 175–96.

19. See Seth Mydans, "Made in Thailand: New Films about Vietnam," *New York Times,* June 4, 1987, p. A19.

20. Michael Reese, "Black Humor Goes to War," *Newsweek,* January 4, 1985, pp. 50–51.

21. See John Culhane, "Robin Williams Belts out Verbal Jazz in Vietnam," *New York Times,* December 20, 1986, p. 34.

22. Pilger, "Vietnam, Another Hollywood Fairy Story," p. 23.

23. For an interesting analysis of this issue, see Robert Gooding-Williams, ed., *Reading Rodney King, Reading Urban Uprising* (New York: Routledge, 1993); see also Jan Pieterse, *White on Black: Images of Africa and Blacks in Western Popular Culture* (New Haven: Yale University Press, 1992); and Sander Gilman, *Difference and Pathology: Stereotypes of Sexuality, Race, and Madness* (Ithaca: Cornell University Press, 1985).

24. Judith Butler, "Endangered/Endangering: Schematic Racism and White Paranoia," in Gooding-Williams, *Reading Rodney King,* p. 15.

25. Toni Morrison, *Playing in the Dark* (Cambridge: Harvard University Press, 1992), p. 82.

26. David Morley and Kevin Robins, "Spaces of Identity: Communications Technologies and Reconfiguration of Europe," *Screen* 30:4 (1989), p. 31.

27. Ibid.

28. For diverse analyses of post-Fordism and its ramifications

for politics, culture, and the global economy, see Ash Amin, *Post-Fordism: A Reader* (London: Basil Blackwell, 1994).

29. Hilary Radner, "Pretty Is as Pretty Does: Free Enterprise and the Marriage Plot," in Jim Collins, Hilary Radner, and Ava Preacher Collins, eds., *Film Theory Goes to the Movies* (New York: Routledge, 1993), p. 67.

30. Suzanne Moore is right in arguing, in her article "Power Play," *New Statesman and Society,* May 18, 1990, p. 47, that *Pretty Woman* is despicable precisely because the violence it perpetrates against women is disguised in the "innocence" of romance. "Yet, who will condemn *Pretty Woman,* which is full of the worst kind of lie where male economic dominance is twisted into pure romance? This is the long slow violence which turns the imbalance of power between the sexes from being part of the problem into being part of the solution. Which is about as close as I want to get to a definition of misogyny."

31. Radner, "Pretty Is as Pretty Does," p. 62.

32. Abigail Solomon-Godeau, *Photography at the Dock* (Minneapolis: University of Minnesota Press, 1991), p. xxii.

33. On the politics of pedagogy and representation, see Henry A. Giroux, *Disturbing Pleasures: Learning Popular Culture* (New York: Routledge, 1994); Henry A. Giroux, *Channel Surfing* (New York: St. Martin's, 1997).

34. See Simon, "Forms of Insurgency."

5

TURNING AMERICA INTO
A TOY STORE

The specific appeal of Disneyland, Disney films and products—family entertainment—comes from the contagious appeal of innocence.

—Michael Eisner

The Southern Baptist Convention in June 1997 generated a lot of media attention when it called for a boycott of the Disney Company for promoting "immoral ideologies such as homosexuality." The Southern Baptists were angry because Disney sponsors "Gay Days" at its theme parks, provides health benefits to the domestic partners of gay employees, and publishes books about growing up gay. According to Herb Hilliger, a convention spokesman, the last straw came in April when the lead character of the sitcom *Ellen* had the audacity to come out as a lesbian on the Disney-owned ABC.[1]

The Baptists got it right in assuming that something was amiss in Disney's image as an icon of clean childhood fun and healthy family entertainment, but they got the reason wrong. Disney should not be condemned because it refuses to endorse homophobic practices in its labor operations and television programming but because its pretense to innocence camouflages a powerful cultural force and corporate monolith—in Eric Smoodin's words "a kind of Tennessee Valley Authority of leisure and entertainment"[2]—that commodifies culture, sanitizes historical memory, and constructs children's identities exclusively within the ideology of consumerism.

Far from being a model of moral leadership and social responsibility, Disney monopolizes media power, limits the free flow of information, and undermines substantive public debate. Disney poses a serious threat to democracy by corporatizing public space and by limiting the avenues of public expression and choice.[3] Disney does not, of course, have the power to launch armies, dismantle the welfare state, or eliminate basic social programs for children; Disney's influence is more subtle and pervasive. It shapes public consciousness through its enormous economic holdings and cultural power. Michael Ovitz, a former Disney executive, says that Disney is not a company but a nation-state, exercising vast influence over global constituencies.[4] Influencing large facets of cultural life, Disney ranks fifty-first in the Fortune 500 and controls ABC, numerous TV and cable stations, five motion picture studios, 728 Disney Stores, multimedia companies, and two major publishing houses. In 1997, Disney pulled in a record $22.7 billion in revenues from all of its divisions.[5] Not content to peddle conservative ideologies, it now provides prototypes for developing American culture and civility, including a model town, a prototype school system, and the Disney Institute, where it offers the intellectually curious vacations organized around learning skills in gardening, radio and television production, cinema, fitness regimens, and cooking.

Disney has always understood the connection between

learning and power and their relationship to culture and politics. As one of the most powerful media conglomerates in the world, Disney promotes cultural homogeneity and political conformity, waging a battle against individuals and groups who believe that central to democratic public life is the necessity of democratizing cultural institutions, including the mass media. Extravagant, feature-length animated films, theme parks, and the Disnification of West Forty-second Street in New York City certainly may have entertainment and educational value, but they cannot be used as a defense for Disney's stranglehold on the message and image business, its stifling of unpopular opinions, or its relentless corporatizing of civic discourse—all of which undermine democratic cultural and political life.

What the Southern Baptists missed was that Disney's alleged transgression of family values and morality has nothing to do with its labor policies or representations of gays and lesbians. On the contrary, Disney's threat to civic life comes from its role as a transnational communications industry capable of ideological influence over vast segments of the American cultural landscape and, increasingly, the rest of the world. In the "magic kingdom," choice is about consumption, justice is rarely the outcome of social struggles, and history is framed nostalgically in the benevolent, patriarchal image of Walt Disney himself. In the animated world of Disney's films, monarchy replaces democracy as the preferred form of government, people of color are cast as either barbarous or stupid, and young Kate Moss–like waifs such as Pocahontas, Megara in *Hercules,* and Mulan support the worst kind of gender divisions and stereotypes. Combining economic control with pedagogical influence, Disney has become a major cultural player in American life, and the first casualties of its dominance in popular culture are, of course, the most defenseless—children.

More insidiously, Disney uses its much-touted commitment to wholesome entertainment to market toys, clothes, and gadgets to children. Beneath Disney's self-proclaimed role as an icon of American culture lies a powerful educational apparatus that provides ideologically loaded fantasies. Walt Disney imagineers have little to do with "dreaming" a better world or even commenting on the world that today's kids actually inhabit. On the contrary, fantasy for Disney has no basis in reality, no sense of real conflicts, struggles, joys, and social relations. Fantasy is a marketing device, a form of hype rooted in the logic of self-interest and consumption.

Disney's view of children as consumers has little to do with innocence and a great deal to do with corporate greed and the realization that behind the vocabulary of family fun and wholesome entertainment is the opportunity for teaching children that critical thinking and civic action in society are far less important to them than the role of passive consumers. Eager to reach children under twelve, "who shell out $17 billion a year in gift and allowance income and influence $172 billion more spent by their parents," Disney relies on consultants such as the marketing researcher James McNeal to tap into such a market.[6] McNeal can barely contain his enthusiasm about targeting children as a fertile market and argues that the "world is poised on the threshold of a new era in marketing and that . . . fairly standardized multinational marketing strategies to children around the globe are viable."[7] For McNeal and his client, the Walt Disney Company, kids are reduced to customers, and serving the public good is an afterthought.

In its search for new markets and greater profits, Disney presents its films, theme parks, and entertainment as objects of consumption rather than as spheres of participation. Art in the Magic Kingdom becomes a spectacle designed to create new markets, commodify children, and provide vehicles for merchandizing its commodities. Films such as *The Lion King, Pocahontas, The Hunchback of Notre Dame, Hercules,* and *Mulan* are used to convert J. C. Penney, Toys 'R Us, McDonald's, and numerous other retailers into Disney merchandising outlets. But the real commercial blitz is centered in Disney's own marketing and distribution network, which includes the Disney Store, the Disney Channel, *Disney* magazine, Disneyland, and Walt Disney World.[8]

Given the recent media attention on the exploitation of children and young adults over the use of heroin chic in the fashion industry, the sexualization of young girls in the world of high-powered models, and the eroticization of six-year-olds in children's beauty pageants, it is surprising that there is little public outcry over the baleful influence Disney exercises on children. The Southern Baptists and the general public appear indifferent to Disney's role in attaching children's desires and needs to commodities, convincing these children that the only viable public space left in which to experience themselves as agents is in the toy sections of Wal-Mart or the local Disney Store.

Growing up corporate has become a way of life for American youth. Corporate mergers, such as Disney's buyout of ABC, consolidate corporate control of assets and markets. An accelerated commercialism has become apparent in all aspects of life, including the "commercialization of public schools, the renaming of public streets for commercial sponsors, Janis Joplin's Mercedes pitch, restroom advertising, and [even the marketing] of an official commercial bottled water of a papal visit."[9] Accountable only to the bottom line of profitability, companies such as Disney carpet bomb their audiences with aired commercials and magazine ads.[10] Michael Jacobson and Laurie Ann Mazur esti-

mate that each day, "260 million Americans are exposed to at least 18 billion display ads in magazines and daily newspapers [as well as] 2.6 million radio commercials, 300,000 television commercials and 500,000 billboards."[11]

Although it is largely recognized that market culture exercises a powerful role educationally in mobilizing desires and shaping identities, it is still a shock that an increasing number of pollsters report that young people, when asked to provide a definition for democracy, refer to "the freedom to buy and consume whatever they wish, without government restriction."[12] Growing up corporate suggests that, as commercial culture replaces public culture, the language of the market becomes a substitute for the language of democracy; at the same time, the primacy of commercial culture has an eroding effect on civil society as the function of schooling shifts from creating a "democracy of citizens [to] a democracy of consumers."[13] One consequence is that consumerism appears to be the only kind of citizenship being offered. Confusing democracy with the market does more than hollow out those public spheres whose roots are moral rather than commercial; it also fails to heed an important insight expressed by Federico Mayor, the director general of UNESCO, who argues that "you cannot expect anything from uneducated citizens except unstable democracy."[14]

Disney's role as the arbiter of children's culture may seem abstract when expressed in these terms, but in the aftermath of the promotional blitz for Disney's animated film *Hercules,* the mix of educational strategy and greed was brought home to me with great force. My three boys were watching television news clips of the Disney parade in New York City and were in awe of Disney's extravaganza, which held up traffic in thirty city blocks and pulled out every stop in the creation of glitz, pomp, and spectacle. Of course, they couldn't wait to see the film, buy the spin-off toys, and be the first on their block to wear a Hercules pin. "Pin? What pin?" I asked. I hadn't watched the promotional ad carefully enough. It seems that Disney was providing a special showing of the film *Hercules* on June 21, 1997, a few weeks before its general release. But to get a ticket for the special showing, I (and thousands of other parents) had to go to an authorized Disney Store to buy a box, for seven dollars, that contained a ticket, a pin of one of the characters in the film, a brochure, and a tape of a song in the show, sung by Michael Bolton. Disney was in full force in this instance making sure that every kid, including my own, knew that along with the film came stuffed animals, figurines, backpacks, lunch boxes, tapes, videos, and a host of other gadgets soon to be distributed by Mattel, Timex, Golden Books, and other manufacturers of children's culture. Once again, children become the reserve army of consumers for the industrial state. (Not to mention that Disney's products are sold by companies like Mattel, Hasbro, and others that routinely exploit workers in China, Mexico, Indonesia, and elsewhere.

Disney is shameless in turning the film hero Hercules into an advertisement for spin-off merchandise. Once Hercules proved himself through his brave deeds, Disney turned him into a public relations hero with a marketable trade name for products such as Air Hercules sneakers, toy figurines, and action-hero dolls, all of which can be bought in an emporium modeled shamelessly in the film after a Disney Store. Michael Eisner claims that the film is about building character, about "sophisticated style, and [about] a hip sense of humor."[15] Clearly, "character" has less to do with developing a sense of integrity and civic courage than with getting a laugh and building name recognition in order to sell consumer goods. *Hercules* suggests that the Dis-

ney dream factory is less a guardian of childhood innocence than a predatory corporation that views children's
imaginations as simply another resource for amassing earn-
ings.[16]

As market culture permeates the social order, it threatens
to cancel out the tension between market values and those
values representative of civil society that cannot be measured in commercial terms but that are critical to democracy, values such as justice, freedom, equality, health, re-
spect, and the rights of citizens as equal and free human
beings. Without such values, students are relegated to the
role of economic machines, and the growing disregard for
public life is left unchecked.

History is clear about the dangers of unbridled corporate
power in the United States. Four hundred years of slavery
(ongoing through unofficial segregation), the exploitation
of child labor, the sanctioning of cruel working conditions
in coal mines and sweatshops, and the destruction of the
environment have all been fueled by the law of maximiz-
ing profits and minimizing costs, especially when there has
been no countervailing power from civil society to hold
such powers in check. This is not to suggest that corporations are the enemy of democracy but to highlight the importance of a strong democratic civil society that sets limits
to the reach and effects of corporate culture. John Dewey
was right: democracy requires work.[17]

Alex Molnar is also right in warning educators, parents,
and others that the market does not provide "guidance on
matters of justice and fairness that are at the heart of a democratic civil society."[18] The power of corporate culture,
when left to its own devices, respects few boundaries and
even fewer basic social needs, such as a safe food supply,
universal health care, and safe forms of transportation.
Moreover, as multinational corporations become more

powerful by amassing assets and increasing their control over the circulation of information in the media, there remains little countervailing discourse about the role they play in undermining the principles of justice and freedom and in limiting the range of views at the center of our civic institutions.[19] This is particularly true for public schools, whose function, in part, is to teach about the importance of critical dialogue, debate, and decision making in a participatory democracy.[20]

What strategies are open to educators, parents, and others who want to challenge the corporate Disney barons who are shaping children's culture in the United States? First, it must become clear that Disney is not merely about peddling entertainment; it is also about politics, economics, and education. Corporations such as Disney do not give a high priority to social values, except to manipulate and exploit them. With every product that Disney produces, whether for adults or children, there is the accompanying commercial blitzkrieg aimed at excessive consumerism, selfishness, and individualism. This commercial onslaught undermines and displaces the values necessary to define ourselves as active and critical citizens rather than as consumers.

Moreover, driven by the imperatives of profit, Disney and other megacorporations reward ideas, messages, and values that are supportive of the status quo while marginalizing dissident views. A vibrant democratic culture is not served well by shrinking the range of critical public spheres, discourses, and relations necessary for the full, active participation of its citizens in shaping political culture. Disney, Time-Warner, and other corporate giants constitute a media system or national entertainment state that has "negative implications for the exercise of political democracy: it encourages a weak political culture that makes depoliticization, apathy and selfishness rational choices for the citizenry, and it permits the business and commercial interests that actually rule U.S. society to have inordinate influence over media content."[21]

Second, battles must be waged on numerous fronts to make clear the political, economic, and cultural influence that media industries such as Disney exercise in a democratic society. This suggests at the least the hard pedagogical and political work of getting the word out that "fewer than ten transnational media conglomerates dominate much of our media; fewer than two dozen account for the overwhelming majority of our newspapers, magazines, films, television, radio and books."[22] Public debate must be waged in numerous venues by academics, teachers, parents, and others over the implications of such media concentration for commercializing public discourse, limiting the range of dissent, limiting access to channels of communication, and shaping national views, desires, and beliefs.

While the traditional liberal response to such media concentration has been the traditional liberal call for regulation, progressives must interrogate the limits of such regulation and press for more radical structural changes. Educators, parents, community groups, and others must call into question existing structures of corporate power in order to make the democratization of media culture central to any reform movement. In part, this suggests taking ownership away from the media giants and spreading these resources among many sites in order to make media culture diffuse and accountable. Such monopolies are a political and cultural toxin, and their hold can be broken through broad-based movements using a variety of strategies, including public announcements, sit-ins, teach-ins, and boycotts, to raise public consciousness, promote regulation, and encourage antitrust legislation aimed at breaking up media monopolies and promoting the noncommercial, nonprofit public sphere.[23]

Progressives also need to press for a combination of state-supported, nonprofit, noncommercial television, radio, journalism, and other cultural formations impervious to the pernicious influence of advertisers and corporate interests. At the same time, progressives must be vigilant in not tying public broadcasting to state control.[24] In 1990, the federal government spent an estimated "\$171 million on the National Endowment for the Arts, less than it allocated to the Pentagon for military bands."[25] Clearly, any commitment on the part of the government to cultural democracy must be tied to subsidies that allow independent media to flourish outside of the commercial sphere.

Defending media democracy is not tantamount to demanding that schools teach media literacy, nor is it simply about providing students with more choices in what they watch, hear, buy, or consume. These issues are important but become meaningless if abstracted from issues of institutional and economic power and how it is used, organized, controlled, and distributed. For example, as important as it is to teach students to learn how to read ads critically in order to understand the values and worldviews the ads are selling, it is not enough. Such literacy should not be limited to matters of textual interpretation or to the recognition that media culture is about business rather than entertainment. Parents, educators, and others need to actively question the manufactured myths, lifestyles, and values created by media giants like Disney to sell identities and increase profits.

Media literacy as a political commodity and pedagogical strategy means teaching strategies of interpretation and strategies of social transformation. As a form of political education, media literacy teaches students how to interpret critically the knowledge, values, and power that are produced and circulated through diverse technologies and public spaces while linking such understanding to broader public discourses that invoke the interrelated nature of theory, understanding, and social change. Makani Themba claims that "media literacy must be more than helping children and families take a discerning look at media. We need to work together to forge new partnerships—new covenants—that address corporate irresponsibility and government neglect. We must not only talk with kids and admonish them to stay on track, we must also hold those businesses accountable who prey on our young people."[26]

Children are growing up in a world shaped by a visual culture under the control of a handful of megacorporations that influence much of what young people learn. We need a new language to address these forms of power and their interlocking systems that dominate the production of knowledge. Against the power of a global culture industry driven by commercialism and commodification, it is crucial that we reclaim the language of critical citizenry, democracy, and social values. Financial and institutional support is necessary to develop those public cultures and spaces in which open deliberation, critical debate, and public education are not undermined by the imperatives of big business and advertising but are shaped by those social and critical values necessary for building democratic communities, identities, and social relations. This suggests curbing the power of big media and weakening the influence of advertising in shaping cultural life. Media giants such as Disney must be challenged. Disney has created a national entertainment state capable of exercising unchecked corporate power within "the injustices of an unregulated global economy."[27]

The time has come to challenge Disney's self-proclaimed

role as a purveyor of "pure entertainment" and take seriously Disney's educational role in producing ideologically
loaded fantasies aimed at teaching children selective roles,
values, and cultural ideals.[28] Progressive educators and
other cultural workers need to pay attention to how the
pedagogical practices produced and circulated by Disney
and other mass-media conglomerates organize and control
a circuit of power that extends from producing cultural
texts to shaping the contexts in which they will be taken
up by children and others.

In addition, as a principal producer of popular culture,
Disney's films, television programs, newscasts, and other
forms of entertainment should become objects of critical
analysis, understanding, and intervention both inside and
outside of schools. It is almost a commonplace that most of
what students learn today is not in the classrooms of public
schools or, for that matter, in the classrooms of higher education but in electronically generated media spheres. Con-
sequently, students need to acquire the knowledge and
skills to become literate in multiple symbolic forms so as to
be able to read critically the various cultural texts to which
they are exposed. This is not to suggest that we should junk
the canon for Disney studies but to suggest that we refash-
ion what it is that students learn in relation to how their
identities are shaped outside of academic life.

Students need to become multiply literate and focus on
diverse spheres of learning. The issue of what is valuable
knowledge is not reducible to the tired either/or culture
war arguments that pervade the academy. Maybe the more
interesting questions point in different directions: What is
it that students need to learn to live in a substantive democracy; to read critically in various spheres of culture; to
engage those traditions of the past that continue to shape
how we think about the present and the future; and to criti-

cally analyze multiple texts for the wisdom they provide and the maps they draw that guide us toward a world that is more multicultural, diverse, and democratic?

Students need to learn how to produce their own newspapers, records, television programs, music videos, and whatever other technology is necessary to link knowledge and power with pleasure and the demands of public life. But for such skills to become useful, they must be connected to the larger project of radical democracy and technological justice, that is, to the struggle for local communities to have universal access to the internet, public broadcasting, and the institutional spaces for theater, newspaper, and magazine productions. Put simply, young people need access to subsidized, noncommodified public spheres that allow their artistic, intellectual, and critical talents to flourish.

Corporate power is pervasive and will not give up its resources willingly. Resistance to dominant corporate culture means developing pedagogical and political strategies that both educate and transform, that build alliances while recognizing different perspectives, and that foreground the struggle over democracy as the central issue. Any attempt to challenge media giants such as Disney demands linking cultural politics with policy battles. Changing consciousness must become part of practical politics designed to change legislation, to reorganize and distribute resources, and to redefine the relationship between pedagogy and social justice, between knowledge and power. Building alliances is especially important, and progressives need a new language for bringing together cultural workers that ordinarily have not worked well together. This suggests finding ways to organize educators at all levels of schooling in order to gain control over those pedagogical forces that shape our culture. And this means addressing the pedagogical force of those cultural industries that have supplanted the school as society's most important educational force.

There is also the imperative to reinvigorate unionized labor, whose funds and power can help us fight for social justice, particularly through gaining access to the media as a site for public pedagogy, especially as that pedagogy shapes the lives of young people.[29] Unions must be convinced that the struggle over wages, better working conditions, and health benefits becomes more meaningful and just when linked to the broader discourse of democracy and its impact upon those populations who are often marginalized.

Finally, we need to organize those who inhabit cultural spheres that produce, circulate, and distribute knowledge but who seem removed from matters of education, pedagogy, and cultural politics. Artists, lawyers, social workers, and others need to acknowledge their role as public intellectuals engaged in a pedagogy that offers them an opportunity to join with other cultural workers to expand the noncommodified public space.

These are highly general suggestions, but they offer a starting point for making the pedagogical more political and for making hope the basis for practical resistance. Disney got its eye blackened when its attempt in 1995 to create a theme park on a historical Virginia landmark was successfully resisted by active citizens. This victory, while modest, suggests that dominant power is never total, resistance is possible, and pedagogical work is fundamental to the struggle for social justice. While we cannot underestimate the political power and cultural force of corporations such as Disney in undermining democratic public life and in turning every aspect of daily life into either a commercial or an appendage of the market, we must continually make visible the threat such corporations pose to democracy everywhere.

Challenging the ideological underpinnings of Disney's construction of common sense is the first step in understanding the ways in which corporate culture has refashioned the relationship between education and entertainment, on the one hand, and institutional power and cultural politics, on the other. It is also a way of rewriting and transforming such a relationship by putting democracy before profits and entertainment and by defining such a project within the parameters of a broad political and pedagogical struggle. The aims of this struggle are (1) creating public spheres that educate for critical consciousness, (2) closing the gap in wealth and property between the rich and poor, and (3) providing the resources for creating a democratic media linked to multiple public spheres.

NOTES

1. Lori Sharn, "Southern Baptists Denounce Disney, Urge Boycott," *USA Today,* June 19, 1997, p. 1A.

2. Eric Smoodin, "How to Read Walt Disney," in Smoodin, ed., *Disney Discourse: Producing the Magic Kingdom* (New York: Routledge, 1994), p. 3.

3. For an analysis of the emerging "national entertainment state," along with a chart that tracks the acquisitions of four major media conglomerates, including Disney, see Mark Crispin Miller and Janine Jaquet Biden, "The National Entertainment State," *Nation,* June 3, 1996, pp. 23–26. See also Mark Crispin Miller, "Free the Media," *Nation,* June 3, 1996, pp. 9–15.

4. Peter Bart, "Disney's Ovitz Problem Raises Issues for Showbiz Giants," *Daily Variety,* December 16, 1996, p. 1.

5. Figures from *The Walt Disney Company 1997 Annual Report* (Burbank, Calif.: Walt Disney Company, 1997).

6. Andrea Adelson, "Children's Radio Pioneer Is Challenged by Disney," *New York Times,* July 21, 1997, p. D10.

7. James U. McNeal, *Kids as Customers: A Handbook of Marketing for Children* (New York: Lexington Books, 1992).

8. With properties in a variety of markets, Disney can generate enormous profits from these outlets even if an animated film does not do well at the box office. For instance, Robert McChesney points out that "the animated films *Pocahontas* and *Hunchback of Notre Dame* were only marginal successes at the box office, with roughly $100 million in gross US revenues, but both films will generate close to $500 million in profit for Disney, once it has exploited all other venues: TV shows on its ABC network and cable channels, amusement park rides, comic books, CD-ROMs, CDs, and merchandising (through 600 Disney retail stores)." "Making Media Democratic," *Boston Review* 23:3–4 (1998), p. 4.

9. George R. Wright, *Selling Words: Free Speech in a Commercial Culture* (New York: New York University Press, 1997), p. 181.

10. McChesney uses the term "commercial carpet bombing" and argues that "advertising should be strictly regulated or removed from all children's programming." "Making Media Democratic," pp. 6–7.

11. Don Hazen and Julie Winokur, eds., *We the Media* (New York: New Press, 1997), p. 40.

12. Wright, *Selling Words,* p. 182.

13. Gerald Grace, "Politics, Markets, and Democratic Schools: On the Transformation of School Leadership," in A. H. Halsey, Hugh Lauder, Philip Brown, and Amy Stuart Wells, eds., *Education: Culture, Economy, Society* (New York: Oxford University Press, 1997, p. 315.

14. Burton Bollag, "Unesco Has Lofty Aims for Higher-Education Conference, but Critics Doubt Its Value," *Chronicle of Higher Education,* September 4, 1998, p. A76.

15. Michael Eisner, with Tony Schwartz, *Work in Progress* (New York: Random House, 1998), p. 414.

16. For an excellent critical analysis of how toys limit the imaginations of children, see Stephen Kline, *Out of the Garden:*

Toys and Children's Culture in the Age of TV Marketing (London: Verso, 1993). For an analysis of how marketing is spreading to different populations of youth in a variety of sites, see Larry Armstrong, "Is Madison Avenue Taking 'Get 'Em While They're Young' Too Far?" *Business Week,* June 30, 1997, pp. 62–67. For a critique of the commercialization of public schools, see Alex Molnar, *Giving Kids the Business* (Boulder, Colo.: Westview, 1996).

17. John Dewey, *Democracy and Education* (New York: Free Press, 1916).

18. Molnar, *Giving Kids the Business,* p. 17.

19. Andre Schiffrin, the director of the New Press, brilliantly illustrates how the takeover of the book publishing industry by conglomerates is eliminating books that cannot be made into films or television series or achieve instant blockbuster status. The result has been that important literary works, scholarly books, books that are critical of corporate power, and others that do not fit into the for-profit formula driving the big publishing houses simply do not get published. This is no small matter, considering that independent and university publishers constitute only about 1 percent of the total sales in book publishing. See "Public-Interest Publishing in a World of Conglomerates," *Chronicle of Higher Education,* September 4, 1998, pp. B4–B5.

20. Benjamin Barber, "The Making of McWorld," *New Perspectives Quarterly* 12:4 (1995), pp. 13–17.

21. Robert W. McChesney, *Corporate Media and the Threat to Democracy* (New York: Seven Stories Press, 1997), p. 7.

22. McChesney, "Making Media Democratic."

23. See Mark Crispin Miller, "Free the Media," *Nation,* June 3, 1996, pp. 9–15; see also John Keane, *The Media and Democracy* (London: Polity, 1991); Noam Chomsky, *Manufacturing Consent* (New York: Pantheon, 1988); George Gerbner, Hamid Mowlana, and Herbert I. Schiller, *What Conglomerate Control of Media Means for America and the World* (Boulder, Colo.: Westview, 1996).

24. Robert W. McChesney argues that this is not a call to abolish the commercial media but to make sure that it is not the dominant sector of the culture industry. Moreover, if the dominant

sector is to be nonprofit, noncommercial, and accountable to the public, the commercial media should have a 1 percent tax levied on them to subsidize the noncommercial sector. He also calls for the leasing of spectrum space. These combined taxes, he estimates, would bring in over $3 billion in revenue—no small matter, considering that in 1997 the total federal subsidy to public broadcasting was $250 million. See McChesney, *Corporate Media and the Threat to Democracy,* p. 67.

25. Sut Jhally, "Moving beyond the American Dream," in Hazen and Winokur, *We the Media,* p. 41.

26. Makani Themba, "Holding the CEO's Accountable," in Hazen and Winokur, *We the Media,* p. 88.

27. Eyal Press, "Barbie's Betrayal: The Toy Industry's Broken Workers," *Nation,* December 30, 1996, p. 12.

28. This argument is used by many media conglomerates. For a devastating critique of this position, see McChesney, *Corporate Media and the Threat to Democracy*; Hazen and Winokur, *We the Media.* Also see Charles Derber, Corporation Nation (New York: St. Martin's Press, 1998).

29. Robert McChesney argues that labor could subsidize nonprofit and noncommercial media without micromanaging them. For such media to flourish, they must remain independent. "We need a system of real public broadcasting, with no advertising, that accepts no grants from corporations or private bodies, and that serves the entire population, not merely those who are disaffected from the dominant commercial system and have to contribute during pledge drives." "Making Media Democratic," pp. 4–5.

INDEX

ABOUT THE AUTHOR

Henry A. Giroux is the well-known author of many books and articles on society, education, politics, and culture. He is the Waterbury Chair Professor of Education at The Pennsylvania State University.